Christmas '03

Dick Walsh

To Dear Elaine

Love
Kathleen..

DICK WALSH REMEMBERED

Selected Columns from **THE IRISH TIMES** 1990-2002

FOREWORD BY
JOHN McGAHERN

AFTERWORD BY GERALDINE KENNEDY

TOWN
HOUSE
DUBLIN

First published in 2003 by

TownHouse, Dublin
THCH Ltd
Trinity House
Charleston Road
Ranelagh
Dublin 6
Ireland

1 2 3 4 5 6 7 8 9 10

A CIP catalogue record for this book is available from the British Library.

ISBN: 1-86059-196-5

Cover design by Anú Design, Tara
Text design and typeset by Kevin Boyle
Printed by Cox & Wyman Ltd, Reading, Berkshire

Contents

Contents

Acknowledgements

The selection of columns was made by Gerry Smyth, a long-time colleague of Dick Walsh. He would like to acknowledge the invaluable assistance of the *Irish Times* library staff, Irene Stevenson and Esther Murnane, and the insightful contributions of John McGahern and Geraldine Kennedy, Editor of *The Irish Times*.

Foreword by John McGahern

DICK WALSH WROTE uncommonly well: he had intelligence and feeling, wit and humour, a gritty, fearless integrity.

Most political columns disappear with the events that brought them into being, yet many of the pieces collected here remain as fresh as on the day they first appeared. This is largely due to the quality of the writing, but a number of other things play a part. In the time that they cover, rapid change was being forced on the institutions that had governed and shaped our lives. Habits of thought, unexamined for so long that they had acquired tacit legitimacy, came under open scrutiny. The simple certainties began to look simple but no longer certain. North and South were unable to ignore either one another or the wider world in which they were set; undreamed of wealth came suddenly to a country long accustomed to poverty and the poor mouth; our first woman president was elected. Reluctantly, it seemed, we were realising that the country was ours at last, while forces honed at home and elsewhere were poised to take it off our hands. All this was observed through the eyes of a fascinating political intelligence that believed passionately in freedom and democracy, its institutions and safeguards. That he also had a social agenda of his own, a vision of what constituted a just society, gave an edge to everything he wrote.

"We need more scepticism (not more cynicism); we need class politics (not a retreat from it); and we need a vigorous opposition that ensures exposure is followed by action.

> "This is not to propose the left's return to the bad old days of half-baked jargon masquerading as Marxism but to suggest a cool, clear look at the way things are in the country."

In any civilised society, he believed, there should be state protection for the weak and disadvantaged, a level below which it was unacceptable to allow people to fall. There should also be curbs on the rich and powerful to prevent them from devouring everything around them; he did not see enterprise and fairness as incompatibles.

> "There is a suggestion that not only are equity and efficiency mutually exclusive, the efficient by the very nature of their enterprise are special cases – are entitled to cut corners.

> "But cutting corners, as we've seen, leads to some riding roughshod over the planning laws, company laws, financial regulations and other controls designed to ensure that in this Republic every citizen is bound by the same code."

The style he forged is highly individual. Mixing the language of the street and field and public house with clear English, it is immediately engaging. The nonchalance is illusory, masking a deadly seriousness. Not surprisingly, from time to time he engaged directly with political language: "If thought corrupts language, then language can also corrupt." He saw Orwell's reference to the effect of Stalinism on western thinking as equally applicable to the 1990s, and he detailed how "the slovenliness of language makes it easier for us to have foolish thoughts".

"Jargon and cliché combine to cover real meanings and so avoid upsetting us by bringing us face to face with reality. The expression used by some American services – 'terminate with extreme prejudice' – was obviously chosen to make killing more acceptable to the squeamish. Every force engaged in killing has its own deadly lingo: the Provisional IRA talks about legitimate targets."

Fellow journalists who worked alongside him, covering elections and conventions or state visits outside the country, speak of the intimidating rigour and pace at which he worked. No report or speech or manifesto went unread, no fact unchecked, every reference was hunted down. His ease when he came to write was based on mastery.

"Paddy Smith of RTÉ announced lately that ostrich farming had begun in England; and he wondered if it might take on here. I was surprised he hadn't noticed: we've been growing our own for years.

"Not, I may add, without success. A foreign correspondent who was here for the general election asked why it was that candidates in Ireland invariably *stood* for office while in the United States and Britain they *ran* for it. The answer of course is that you can't run for anything with your head in the sand; and some of our home-grown ostriches have made it to the top while maintaining this well-known national position."

There are people, especially in Fianna Fáil, who accuse him of bias and animosity towards that party. Walsh himself came from an old Fianna Fáil family in the Clare heartland. As our biggest political party, its grassroots in every corner of the land and with one of the longest records of government in parliamentary democracy, he saw Fianna Fáil, together with the Catholic Church, as the organisation that had the most profound influence on all our lives. In his moving tribute to Jack Lynch, he describes the nature of the party that Lynch joined. In this early innocence, Walsh read the seeds of its later vices. That party, seeing the nation and itself as one, had hardly any need of programmes and rules. Broad national aims were sufficient. Pragmatism was elevated to the point of principle, and policy was whatever the leader said it was, but that was when the leader lived within his means, and words such as patriotism and honour and honesty had meaning. This grew to become a demand that the leader and the party should be unquestioned, he wrote in 1990, "like an overbearing heavyweight in late-night company who cannot see how anyone can take a different view and, in certain circumstances, why anyone should be allowed to do so". The great power and influence Fianna Fáil wielded was the very reason it should be scritinised Walsh believed, and this he did with a clinical savagery, though, at the same time, he was willing to praise individual members and contributions, such as Bertie Ahern's imaginative and courageous response to Northern Ireland.

The mindset was what he hated, its willingness to speak to different audiences in different voices in order to hang on to power at any cost. That the party hadn't the courage to legislate for change was to lead into the sorry moral mazes around contraception, family planning, divorce and abortion – he does not exempt the other parties from this cowardice, but they hadn't anything like the same power – and this moral ambiguity was to surface in other forms in the various tribunals. Dick Walsh takes us through those mazes with a formidable lucidity. During the divorce referendum, when there was much scaremongering that the institution of marriage would collapse if the right to divorce was granted, he argued that the logic of this is "like saying that the existence of coronary units encourages heart attacks". On abortion he writes:

> "The number of women going to Britain for abortions stands at more than 4,000 a year. Since the State refuses to allow clinics here – which would be the most sensible and least hypocritical thing to do – the traffic is bound to continue... When we discuss abortion and related issues, we stand at a crossroads where politics, religion, medicine and law intersect and the woman, who is faced with choice, is in danger of being left alone while gatherings of men, often middle-aged or elderly, some bound by celibacy, argue the toss."

On the North, he saw little to choose between republican and unionist dogmatism. "On either side, whether fired by the Covenant or the Proclamation, only one feeling was stronger than suspicion and fear. It was the unshakeable sense of being right."

When he went to work in the North, he was nettled to discover that his own stereotypical view of the place was matched by a similarly clichéd view of the South as a corrupt, priest-ridden place. Where he saw hope was not in those walled simplicities but in some "who've carried the heaviest workloads – tireless, patient people like Seamus Mallon, Reg Empey, Seamus Close, Monica McWilliams and David Ervine".

In Dick Walsh's company, there was a sense that he spoke out of an accumulated wealth of local knowledge from many parts of the country, the terrain, the people, mentalities, their varied histories and stories and strategies – a present-day that was informed by a long past. I believe it is this quality that gives his columns a depth beyond the events of the day, that gave them their first relevance. This quality is present everywhere, and is probably most visible in the piece he wrote on the Famine.

He recalled the simple myth we all grew up with – of grain being exported to pay the rack-rents while the people starved – another vague episode in the terrible history of Irish nationalism and race suffering. Many times in the course of the columns, he turns back to Clare and his influential father, the National School teacher. He tells of accompanying him fifty years ago when, after school, he visited old people collecting the folklore of East Clare. They often visited two brothers, Con and Solomon O'Neill, who were in their eighties and nineties. The brothers were most forthcoming about holy wells and pattern days and the various activities of the Clare fairies but, when asked about the Famine, they would say only that their family had nothing to do with it.

This echoed a larger silence. He recalled, then, his excitement when the various works of scholarship, particularly those of Comac Ó Gráda, came out, enabling him to see the past not only in its suffering but also in its complexity. Visiting his aunt with this knowledge years later, he enquired about the brothers' reticence. "She pointed to a field by a stream we knew as the Sandy River and said people went there to eat the clover and a type of sorrel which grew between the woods and the Shannon. When I asked who they were she said: 'Mountainy people. Poor ould *spailpíns*. They used to find them dead in the ditches.'"

The *spailpíns* were the poorest of the poor, landless labourers: it was the class system that decided who survived, and even prospered, and who died. The enemy was not just the absentee landlords or English landlords, but landlords of *whatever* nationality or religion who used the system for exploitation.

Dick Walsh began his career on the desk of the *Clare Champion* and, in the best sense of the word, remained a local reporter all his life. The local, when the walls are taken away, becomes the universal. He spent his career removing such walls – walls of lies and violence, prejudice and certainty, privilege and deprivation, silence and bullying. The list is endless.

I had the pleasure of his friendship for many years. This is irrelevant here other than to say that the man and his writing were of one piece. He spoke always in his own voice, even to strangers. His later years were afflicted with illness and disability, which he carried with such extraordinary lightness that he gave heart to others. With a smile he would tell how as he waited for his taxi on D'Olier Street, bent over because of his illness, a woman would stop to help him search for coins or whatever he was missing on the pavement.

He was wonderful company and great fun, and he loved to talk. He spoke almost as well as he wrote, with a beautiful rhythmic phrasing. Unlike many who love to talk, he listened intently, and he had the habit of repose. Out of that repose or silence he would sometimes chant mischievously, "Love-ly peop-le... Plen-ty of mon-ey... *No* man-ners."

John McGahern
August 2003

Doublespeak of modern English usage

"A man may take to drink because he deems himself to be a failure, and then fail all the more completely because he drinks. It is rather the same thing that is happening to the English language. It becomes ugly and inaccurate because our thoughts are foolish, but the slovenliness of our language makes it easier for us to have foolish thoughts."

THIS IS FROM George Orwell's essay 'Politics and the English Language' which appeared in 1946, the year after *Animal Farm* was published. Orwell was in a pessimistic mood. During the war intellectuals generally, and specifically those of the left, had allowed their independence to be undermined and they were showing no sign of recovering their critical faculties.

The war effort had demanded a temporary suspension of judgement in the interests of the struggle for democracy. Now, when democracy called for clear and critical appraisal, the habits of half-truth or silence had taken hold. The left either refrained from criticism of the Soviet Union or made excuses for its excesses. At home (that is to say in Britain), there was a tendency to assume that nothing could be done, which led people into the intellectual cul-de-sac of political quietism.

Orwell fought the supporters of Stalinism as he had fought against fascism. Today, in the continuing movement towards democracy in Eastern Europe and the Soviet Union, the themes of *Animal Farm* and *1984* are repeated more eloquently than they were by the crude proponents of the Cold War.

The cold warriors took Orwell's work for companion pieces to that of lesser men, writers who made a good thing of their defection from the left. People whose books might have been called *I was a Teenage Communist.*

The lessons of *Animal Farm* and *1984* are also relevant to the new crusaders who believe in a world of unfettered market forces and international organisations which may prove as impervious to the needs of those who serve them – as labour forces or consumers – as the now-breaking or broken apparatus of totalitarian states.

One of Orwell's constant concerns, which is also relevant now, was for the state of the language; and one of his deepest convictions – topical, too because it is notably shared by Vaclav Havel – was that this was a reversible condition, capable of being changed by the exercise of personal responsibility.

"Most people who bother with the matter at all would admit that the English language is in a bad way," Orwell wrote, "but it is generally assumed that we cannot by conscious effort do anything about it." Most people would probably say now that in the past 40 years the state of the language has become considerably worse; and they would almost certainly feel, more strongly than Orwell's contemporaries, their powerlessness in the face of the deterioration.

We have not yet arrived at the stage where Big Brother goes unchallenged and unassailable. And those countries which appeared to have been under his thumb are well on the way to a happy and healthy escape.

But there are Big Brothers, in publishing and broadcasting for example, whom we would ignore at our peril. Doublethink and doublespeak thrive where cant and cliché fill columns and airwaves with imperturbable self-importance.

The language of state control, which had its origins no doubt in egalitarian concern for the citizens, is giving way in Eastern Europe to the language of the marketplace, with its emphasis on efficiency and competition. But the language of state control came to be simplified into a single, crushing message. Obedience was the key and prison or death the alternative. The vocabulary of the marketplace is also being reduced to simple powerful imperatives. Crush or be crushed, and the alternative is at best irrelevance and at worst starvation.

The process by which powerful, sometimes socially damaging or even dangerous messages are driven home could not succeed were it not for what Orwell calls the "slovenliness of language" which "makes it easier for us to have foolish thoughts".

Jargon and cliché combine to cover real meanings and so avoid upsetting us by bringing us face to face with reality. The expression used by some American services – "terminate with extreme prejudice" – was obviously chosen to make killing more acceptable to the squeamish. Every force engaged in killing has its own deadly lingo: the Provisional IRA talks about legitimate targets.

In less dramatic style, politicians, civil servants and journalists cover *their* tracks. As often as not, they do it for convenience, out of laziness or weariness or fear of reaction. The civil servant who writes that something is under active consideration or prepares an equally obfuscating speech for his Minister does not believe that he is telling lies – he is performing a function.

The Minister who laces his speeches with such adjectives as "positive", "constructive" and "fundamental" does not really expect anyone to take him seriously; he is making a noise which, on the tom-tom to the few who care to listen, means: leave it to me, it'll be all right on the night.

And the journalists who write it down and head it up don't much care whether the Minister means it or not. It is easier to swim with the tide. Where some outsiders see conspiracies and ill will, insiders recognise a desire to get home to tea.

Our society is well stocked with handy phrases which will do instead of making sense. In some cases, making sense is the last thing a speaker or writer wants to do: I heard a politician pretend the other day to explain why inter-party talks in Northern Ireland could not be held at this time. The words "agenda" and "parameters" and "fundamental interests" were uttered and repeated like incantations. And like incantations, the whole thing was meaningless; as though there was no urgency about reaching a settlement.

The public recognises what may be termed the lies of the land. People use them regularly in everyday life. Sects are what other people belong to. Morals have to do with sex. Family is a term employed by cute hoors masquerading as village idiots to exclude single parents. Tradition is whatever you believe in yourself.

But both Orwell and Havel point us in the direction of personal responsibility; an unwillingness, in fact, to be fobbed off with the cant and jargon. It's unfortunate that recognising it – and the other tricks of the communications trade – has not become part of the school curriculum, at least at second level.

An Austrian friend told me last week of the practice in at least some schools in his country of including a course on what he called "manipulation". It included simple lessons on the analysis of political speeches, official statements and journalistic accounts (in print or broadcast) of current affairs. We are badly in need of such lessons.

Agriculture can no longer be a sacred cow

TWENTY YEARS AGO, a man called Sicco Mansholt set this country into a fine fury with his plan for agriculture in the Common Market that Ireland was about to join.

Mansholt, who for years held a powerful position in the European Commission and in the early 1970s was briefly its president, was a walking paradox, a farmer and socialist, a visionary whose dream was a federal Europe, an intellectual who believed it was not only possible to subject farming to structural reform, but that in the new Community, it was essential. The trouble as far as this country was concerned was that the reform entailed an orderly withdrawal from the land.

Ireland wasn't the only country where the mere mention of his name was enough to evoke feelings of outrage and terror. I am not sure that we knew of his Friesian farm (he'd had a promising career in politics in the Netherlands), or that he was bronzed by the Sardinian sun under which he sailed his yacht and built a house for his retirement.

If we were unaware of them, these features of his life would simply have added an angry touch to our portrait of the man who was scheming to rob Irish farmers of the things that they and, for that matter, the rest of us held dearest: land and a traditional way of life.

I heard him speak once in the 1960s at a press conference in Amsterdam which was arranged to douse the tempers raised by one of those occasional trade skirmishes between Europe and the United States. This one was about day-old chicks and, as far as I can remember, Bonn's refusal to allow the Americans access to the West German market. It was called The Chicken War.

I remember more vividly my surprise on hearing Mansholt's calm and thoughtful tones. Coming from the west of Ireland and a background that was all rural and half agricultural, it was like listening to some lordly dissertation on the beneficial effects of the Scottish clearances.

To us, the idea that anyone could plan Irish agriculture was almost as outrageous as the fact that the man who proposed to try was a foreigner who had never wrenched a living from a few rushy acres (the stony grey soil of damn nearly everywhere had left us impoverished and that was how we intended to remain, please God).

On reflection, I don't think it would have made much difference if the idea had come from an Irishman. Agriculture, which everyone declared to be our most important industry was, in every sense of the word, a sacred cow. Justin Keating on RTÉ, Michael Dillon in *The Irish Times*, Paddy O'Keeffe in the *Farmer's Journal*, might talk or write about modernising techniques; Macra na Feirme and the National Farmers' Association (predecessor of the IFA) ran valuable programmes of education for young farmers; and the NFA built a lobby that was second only to the Roman Catholic Church when it came to influencing politicians.

No one talked seriously about land use, or as if there were consumers as well as producers scattered about the country. The role of the State was to assist, not to plan or otherwise regulate, the industry. The Minister for Agriculture became the head centre of the farming lobby. No one in the Dáil dared question the cost of agricultural supports or services; and as all but a tiny minority of urban working-class people were rooted in the land, no one outside the Dáil risked the derision that would undoubtedly have greeted any questioning of the status quo.

In theory, Fianna Fáil distinguished between those whom it called ranchers and the majority who were of humbler means. The Labour Party and socialist republicans cherished an ambition to found a republic of workers and small farmers. In practice, no one seriously took issue with a pattern that had taken shape before the passage of the Land Acts at the turn of the century. Land and its ownership was a more potent force than nationalism (the two were linked) and is likely to prove more durable.

The American essayist, H L Mencken, described common attitudes to farmers or husbandmen, as he quaintly called them in the 1920s, when the American industry more closely resembled ours than it does now. The farmer was the salt of the earth; always crying wolf, forever supported but never, never interfered with. Where people in other lines of business would be declared bankrupt and, if they persisted, clapped in irons and sent to debtors' cells, the farmer was clapped on the back, told how much the nation loved him and sent off with a pocketful of subsidies to incur new debts.

Even Irish agriculture no longer wears the mask of Mencken's caricature. EC membership, in spite of the abandonment of the Mansholt Plan (including his farm-modernisation and retirement schemes), brought great opportunities which were sacrificed to short-term gains and radical changes, the benefits of which were not uniformly spread. Raymond Crotty claims that the Common Agricultural Policy has made the rich richer and the poor poorer – the real beneficiaries as he sees it, are the 1 per cent who own half the land. And a dangerously high degree of specialisation in beef and milk now limits the prospect of expansion.

The roses-round-the-door or tweeds-and-sandals versions of Irish country life were never more than figments of nostalgic imagination. The advantages of EC membership, too, were, in many cases, illusory. At least, they were as selectively distributed as the fruits of agriculture had always been: the class differences which had marked rural life for generations were, if anything, sharpened by the direct and indirect impact of EC policy.

But the CAP was never intended to stand alone. The report of the National Economic and Social Council on Ireland in the EC, which was published last August, makes it quite clear that of the four types of agricultural policy – those dealing with price, productivity, structures and programmes outside agriculture – the CAP only dealt with prices.

The rest, which had to do with how well the land is worked, how many people can live on it and what else they may do to supplement their farm incomes, are, as two respected authorities put it, "Irish problems requiring Irish solutions" – a consistent, well-researched, carefully monitored national policy.

In our case, however, a national policy is what we have not got. The official political reaction to any debate on agriculture has always been, like the reaction to Mansholt, defensive, emotional and, in recent years, evasive: the issue is out of our hands, it's for the EC to decide.

Agricultural economists, whose opinions on the finer points and on ultimate solutions may differ widely, appear to agree that in agriculture, as in other areas of social and economic policy, if we don't help ourselves, no one else can or will. And with the accelerating reform of the CAP (of which Ray MacSharry's support-cutting proposal is the latest example), allied to the probable effects of agreements on world trade, the case is urgent.

Brendan Kearney, writing of the MacSharry proposal and the current GATT negotiations in this paper the other day, commented: "With the probability of an eventual agreement on agricultural trade, however comprised and phased, it will have a profound impact on the structure, viability and vitality of the rural economy. It will accelerate the increase in non-viable holdings, severely reduce farm incomes, depress the multiplier effect of agriculture in the economy, reduce employment in the agri-food sector and devalue rural assets."

What Kearney and others are talking about are the potentially traumatic effects of Mansholt without the benefits: a disorderly withdrawal from the land at a time when other sectors are in no state to take up the slack. They are talking about adding to the rural poverty to which the Combat Poverty Agency, the Conference of Major Religious Superiors and other voluntary agencies have called attention. And they are talking about time running out.

I know that urban–rural divisions have been exacerbated by conflicts over taxation. There are those who imagine all farmers to be equally prosperous and equally greedy. And the habit of hanging on to land until it is useless or the owner is at death's door, needs to be broken. There are farmers who are prepared to resist change at any price and politicians who are afraid to recognise that some politically painful decisions will have to be taken – and taken quickly – if we are not to have many more people on the dole for want of a national policy on the State's most important industry.

Few inspired by altruism in Gulf crisis

IT TOOK THE world a week to conclude that George Bush had not ordered his troops into Saudi Arabia out of the goodness of his democratic heart. This was six days longer than it took for everyone to realise that Saddam Hussein's intention had not been to liberate the people of Kuwait from the al Sabbah family.

But it was not until early this week, almost a fortnight after the Gulf crisis began, that it became clear roughly where Ireland stood in relation to that sweating line in the Arabian sand. For while Iraq and the US squared up to each other, to be joined by their closest allies on either side, other countries took their places, not directly behind, but at an angle to the main protagonists.

These minor actors were, as usual, guided to their places on the spokes or tangents of this map by their own political and economic lights, the extent to which they were committed to those in the leading roles or shared their convictions. Some were influenced by their views of what the Bush administration calls the world economic order, others by appeals to the unity and solidarity of the Arab nation. Few were inspired by altruism.

The Irish public watched, at first with fascination. Another international crisis, remote enough to be regarded as a spectacle, called up its quota of barroom strategists; and if some were worried by the risks of tighter oil supplies and rising prices, others simply enjoyed sharing a communal shudder at a threat which neither they nor the Irish Government could really do anything about. The Government had backed the UN resolutions condemning the Iraqi invasion and imposing sanctions; it supported the EC position favouring the restoration of sovereignty to Kuwait. But that, as far as most people were concerned, was that. They were content to go back to their war games in the bar.

There were two groups who were clearly not content. The first, which was small and virtually helpless, was composed of relatives of Irish people who were living in Iraq or Kuwait when the invasion began. It soon became plain that, although they were not under immediate threat, the Iraqi authorities had no intention of letting them go. It also became plain that, with the best will in the world, there was very little the Government could do to relieve the anguish of those at home or the distress of their relatives who were captive in the Middle East.

And it was clear that what little might be done was not being done in a particularly comforting manner. People at first had trouble getting information from the Department of Foreign Affairs; and Gerald Collins' initial attempt at reassurance was, to say the least, not very reassuring. In an RTÉ Radio interview, he turned up the usual clichés about tension and complexity and followed that by saying that, of course, "we could come out with all guns blazing" which seemed not just unlikely but impossible. "Or we could…" Here the Minister tailed off and for a moment there was a telling silence. Do nothing?

His confident claim that the Government had a contingency plan was not accompanied by any hint as to what it might be. He did not say that it was an arrangement to move Irish citizens, with other EC nationals, out of the area if and when a port or airport was opened, which now appears to be what the plan amounts to and, on a practical level, the best that circumstances permit.

Whether the eventual disclosure that the Government distinguishes between the terms of the UN resolutions and the action taken by those engaged in the military build-up and naval blockade will make any difference to the Iraqi treatment of Irish citizens remains to be seen.

How the US may choose to interpret Ireland's strict adherence to UN decisions is another matter. Remember the views expressed by a leading American commentator and echoed by a former Irish ambassador, Sean Donlon, on the "talk is cheap" aspects of Irish foreign policy and popular opinion? Interestingly, a spokesman at the Department of Foreign Affairs pointed out yesterday that the Government had not exactly withheld support from the blockade since it had not been asked to give it.

Much less subtle distinctions are made by the second group which is discontented with the impact on Ireland of events unfolding in the Middle East. These are the supporters of the Irish beef industry and, unlike the relatives of those trapped in Iraq and Kuwait, they are among the most powerful lobbies in the State. To judge by the public responses to their case, they are not getting the political attention – if not the results – they feel to be their due.

Their case is that sales to Iraq – worth about £45 million last year – have been halted by the crisis and that a compensatory deal with Iran – variously valued at anything from £90 million to £140 million – is in danger of being held up or lost if the Government persists in maintaining the EC ban on ministerial visits to Tehran which was imposed in response to the Iranian death sentence on Salman Rushdie, the author of *The Satanic Verses*.

The Iranians want the Minister for Agriculture to break the ban by travelling to their country to complete the deal. The Irish Farmers' Association, pointing to the possibility that farmers may be left with 200,000 cattle on their hands, insists that he should go. The chairman of the association's Livestock Committee, Gerald Smith, who describes the EC's response to the Rushdie threat as an informal agreement, says: "It is not good enough that this kind of nod and wink arrangement should jeopardise such an important deal for Irish farmers." The IFA's President, Allan Gillis, is more diplomatic but no less insistent: "Obviously a certain amount of displacement of Irish trade is inevitable, but unless these current difficulties are ironed out, all future prospects for Irish contracts are at risk."

The Government is desperately seeking a way out. Mr O'Kennedy says he is willing to travel anywhere but unwilling to break the EC ban. He did, however, take a step, which the Foreign Affairs spokesman acknowledged to be uncommon but not unusual, of going to the Iranian Embassy in Dublin to plead with the Taoiseach during the week: no one was prepared to say where it was or what was discussed.

John Bruton, too, intervened with a statement which began: "The announcement of a major Iraqi peace offer to Iran creates a window of opportunity for the Irish diplomatic efforts to clinch the vital beef deal with Iran through a ministerial visit to that country..." But what exactly Iraq's manoeuvring to concentrate its forces on the Saudi Arabian rather than the Iranian border had to do with Ireland's attitude to the Rushdie ban is as mysterious as the Haughey/O'Kennedy meeting and much else in the world of Irish beef exports.

If Mr Smith thinks the EC's affairs are a matter of wink and nod – and the declaration of the Twelve dated February 20th, 1989 proves him wrong – he should try looking nearer home. I asked the Department of Agriculture yesterday exactly how much the Iranian contract was worth, what companies were involved and what, if anything, Mr O'Kennedy and Mr Haughey had to say to each other on the subject. This was the reply:

> "A number of companies would be interested in supplying beef to Iran this year. The exact value of any contracts to be negotiated and the names of the companies involved will be commercial matters. The Minister and the Taoiseach meet regularly to discuss matters of current interest."

Foreign policy is, of course, influenced by trade as well as by politics; and foreign policy often brings advantages, sometimes exacts a price. But policy isn't and shouldn't be made by or on behalf of the beef industry which, by any standards, is a robust and secretive business. If we agree that George Bush is in Saudi Arabia with oil on his mind, should our position be dictated by beef?

The Government rarely makes a stand on civil liberties or is placed in a position where it must defend the interests of Irish citizens abroad. When it happens, they must take precedence over other considerations – and that includes personal loyalties or commitments.

SEPTEMBER 22nd, 1990

Cowardly ignoring the warning bells

IRELAND'S PREDICAMENT IN the 1990s is becoming clearer with every turn of international events and the deepening crisis which faces agriculture at home. It arises from a lack of vision: a clear idea about the kind of society we want and the place it should have in the wider world.

The Government's good news of the week, that we have joined the low inflation members of the European Community, is outweighed by a combination of problems, of which the crisis in agriculture and a growing demand for a clear-cut foreign policy are the most immediate.

To say that they arise from a lack of vision is to do no more than to repeat the warnings issued at increasingly frequent intervals by an impressive range of commentators extending from Professor Joe Lee to the National Economic and Social Council and the contributors to the series of articles in the *The Irish Times* this week on neutrality and the Gulf crisis.

And if political leaders give the impression that they can do little but sit helplessly on the sidelines while international events impinge with ever-deeper effect on Irish affairs, it is because these leaders have chosen to ignore not only the commentators but their own obligation to provide leadership and guidance.

It has been said before, but now bears repetition, that foreign and domestic policies are inextricably linked and both suffer from a chronic lack of coherent debate and the kind of planning which might not provide immunity to external pressure, but which would ensure a greater capacity to resist it.

We are the victims of a haphazard and opportunistic approach to political life at home and abroad which is exemplified by an irresponsible reliance on piecemeal effort – a combination of patchwork and sleight of hand covering political cowardice and an absence of foresight.

I am not using the accusation of cowardice as a form of vulgar abuse. It has been evident in both of the areas which are now a cause for concern: foreign affairs and agriculture. In other words, the parties of all persuasions knew in advance that trouble was brewing; and, with a few honourable exceptions, their members have chosen to ignore the warning bells.

They preferred not to remind the electorate that the day must come when the full obligations of EC and United Nations membership must be met, and instead side-stepped the consequences for foreign policy generally and neutrality in particular.

They preferred not to tell farmers that numbers on the land were bound to fall at an increasing rate unless efficiency was vastly improved. They refrained from telling them that they could not look forever to EC funds to help them out when the going got tough.

They tried to convince themselves – and some of them probably succeeded – that Ireland would always be regarded by the rest of the international community as a special case in much the same way that the farmers would always be specially favoured by the Irish community.

There was more than a hint of this attitude in Ray MacSharry's approach to the difficulties arising from Larry Goodman's problems. It is present in his struggle with other EC commissioners on what might or might not be conceded in the current round of GATT negotiations. Our ministers for agriculture have always seen themselves as, in the final resort, the farmers' men in the Cabinet and the defence of that constituency as their ultimate role.

But the only special cases which succeed in international affairs are those based on compelling rational arguments and reciprocity; on clear evidence that those who help, in whatever form, are ready to help themselves – and acknowledge their responsibilities as well as the obligations of others.

We cannot expect our partners in the EC to accept our claims to exemption on the grounds of neutrality in one area while making special allowance for our interests when joint action is undertaken by the community in relation to third countries.

And we cannot expect other states to show an understanding of policies, such as neutrality, which we are unwilling to define with any degree of precision ourselves.

Some years ago, at a meeting with West German officials in Bonn, a group of Irish journalists took exception to what appeared to be the cavalier attitude which their hosts displayed towards Irish neutrality. The courteous reply of the most forthcoming official was challenging: if we didn't take the policy seriously enough to arrive at a definition – if we couldn't say exactly what it meant to us – how could we ask him to treat it as anything other than an eccentricity?

To judge by the pieces written by my colleagues, Joe Carroll and Sean Flynn, this week, this quizzical attitude persists. And by all accounts it's bolstered by some mysterious distinction between Ireland's performance at official level and the public pronouncements of the Republic's leaders.

We are, it seems, much less reserved about our role in the international community than the politicians – especially those of the present administration – would wish to appear. It could probably be described as being internationalist by stealth.

The reason for this is the habit, now endemic, of trying to talk to different audiences in different tones. Neutrality is, to a large degree, an expression of anti-Britishness – and woe betide the Minister or Taoiseach who appears less than wholesomely anti-British at home (or so runs the Fianna Fáil rule of thumb). Quiet co-operation, like quiet diplomacy, is another matter.

The parties of the left, meanwhile, are content to follow their traditional lines, ignoring the changes in Eastern Europe and in East–West relations as well as the consistent policies of socialist and social-democratic parties in the European Parliament. The President of the Soviet Union may welcome the Secretary General of NATO to Moscow and promise a return visit to NATO headquarters.

In Ireland, we are used to different codes, which prevent us not merely from participating in meetings which discuss security but from attending them as observers. It's a prohibition reminiscent of the long defunct GAA ban which insisted that members of the organisation should not only refrain from playing foreign games but must avoid contamination by seeing them played.

In one of our pieces on foreign policy last month, Lorna Siggins put the dilemma presented by neutrality and EC membership in a nutshell. If Ireland had still held the presidency of the EC when the Gulf crisis occurred, Charles Haughey would have been the community's spokesman on the EC's response to Iraq. What might have happened then is worth thinking about. As it was, we missed the opportunity and the challenge – by six weeks.

Making a statement about ourselves

NOTHING UNDERLINED THE damage that the week's events had inflicted on Irish politics like the anti-climax of the television debate between the presidential candidates on Thursday night.

Of course the limits set by the Constitution make it difficult for anyone to talk about the presidency in anything other than cagey terms – tiptoeing around de Valera's restrictive notion of the office like people afraid of waking the sleeping elders in the room next door.

But, in spite of Olivia O'Leary's attempts to nudge it gently to life, the debate only caught fire when the week's other events intruded on the candidates' cautious circumspection. As Mary Robinson said, on Wednesday next people will be making a statement about Irish society. Unfortunately, it will have as much, if not more, to do with the conduct of political affairs in the crudest sense than with an office which, everyone agrees, ought to be above partisan politics.

Ms Robinson and Austin Currie insist the election will be about our vision of the future and such qualities in the candidates as judgement, integrity, courage and independence. Brian Lenihan invites a judgement on his record and, by implication, on standards of behaviour which many, though not all, members of his party consider to be both normal and appropriate in politics.

The electorate will be choosing a president. The election, to a very large degree, will be about Fianna Fáil and that party's way of doing business – its own, the Government's and ours.

Why every discussion of politics in Ireland should sooner or later focus on Fianna Fáil, its way of doing business and its leadership, is a subject which frustrates many who are outside the party and is a source of considerable perplexity to some who are inside.

But it's the biggest party in the country, with one of the longest records of government in parliamentary democracy. It has been a major influence on our history, education and development. It has had a profound influence on everyone in the State, whether they acknowledge it or not and whether they love or resent it.

Some may feel that, far from being an obsession of the media or Fianna Fáil's political opponents, the party forces its attention on us like an overbearing heavyweight in late-night company who cannot see how anyone can take a different view and, in certain circumstances, why anyone should be allowed to do so.

In a sense when we are talking about the party we are talking about ourselves as a people. So when we are asked to judge how it conducts our business and its own, we are asked to say something quite significant of ourselves.

As we try to unravel the extraordinary events of the week and ask how Mr Lenihan became unstuck, we cannot confine the question to who did what and when and why but how they came to regard it as acceptable to the rest of us.

To this question, Mr Lenihan himself has given no answer. On television he claimed that he, the Tánaiste, had been dismissed from the Cabinet because Charles Haughey wanted to hold the Government together; because, to avoid a general election, he had to give way to the Progressive Democrats. But why was this – the sacking of his deputy and closest ally, his friend of 30 years – the price the Progressive Democrats demanded of Mr Haughey for the preservation of the Government?

Mr Lenihan wasn't asked and didn't say, though no one who had been paying the remotest attention to the presidential campaign or the statements of the Progressive Democrats could have been in any doubt about it.

Mr Lenihan didn't seem to understand this any more than he appeared to understand how his contradictory accounts of events in 1982 could have led to the inevitable conclusion that he was lying – at least in one version and maybe in both.

There had, of course, been some surprise – among journalists as well as politicians – that the Progressive Democrats had taken the position they adopted in the first place. To risk an election when they had jobs in Government and were showing up badly in the polls? On a question of ethics, a point of principle? Good God, it was unheard of.

But if the honourable role of the Progressive Democrats was unexpected in some quarters and had come to be resented as fiercely as their participation in Government, there was another Fianna Fáil reaction to the Lenihan affair which, I suppose, should have been less surprising. It was expressed in many quarters by ministers, deputies, senators, local activists and indeed in some clerical contributions to a debate which, no doubt, will achieve added ferocity over the weekend.

The themes included Mr Currie's arrival from the North, Ms Robinson's attitude to social affairs and the relatively minor offence committed by Mr Lenihan of lying all round.

The candidate summed up one of the themes when he said in Limerick that he was glad to be back with people who knew what Irish politics was all about. The same message, though in a different form, seemed to be at the heart of a confused speech delivered by a Junior Minister, Michael Smith, in Edenderry, Co. Offaly. He roared on about there being no need for Fianna Fáil people, unlike Fine Gaelers, to go to confession before discovering where they stood. (He was later to add to the general confusion by congratulating Mr Lenihan on his resignation in the national interest the day before he was fired.)

Mr Lenihan's tour around the State was punctuated by other contributions in what might mildly be described as an attacking vein – reminiscent of the referendums on divorce and abortion or even the elections of the 1930s. Here are a few examples.

John Browne, a local deputy, an assistant whip and member of the Committee on Procedure and Privileges, said in Wexford: "[Mary Robinson] is pro-divorce, pro-contraception and pro-abortion. Is she going to have an abortion referral clinic in Áras an Uachtaráin? That's what I'd like to know."

Then, according to the report in the *Wexford People*, he added a bad joke about "Chicken Currie", of which the paper said "in other circumstances, it might have raised a giggle on a drunken Saturday night, but this time it raised the rafters".

In Kilkenny, Mr Lenihan called for a win in good Kilkenny hurling style and Senator Michael Lanigan continued the metaphor:

> "On election day we want to see Fine Gael blood flowing and Labour and Workers' Party blood. They have come from the gutters to the sewers to beat Brian Lenihan. And you all know that the only people who live in the sewer are rats."

In Mayo, a county councillor, Padraic Gavin, sent out a letter asking Fianna Fáil members: "Do you... want to see someone other than a Fianna Fáil person President of Ireland? Do you want as President a lady who represents those who tried to foist abortion, among other undesirable things, on the Irish people?" The letter was issued in Oireachtas envelopes.

When the going gets tough, Fianna Fáil goes for the clerical vote, what the political scientist Tom Garvin calls cultural defenderism. And during Mr Lenihan's excursion to the centre of Dublin on the day after his dismissal, supporters were heard to say that nuns had told them only that morning that "St Peter denied Our Lord three times and still He chose him to be the head of the Church". I thought this a little whimsical on our reporter's part until I discovered the same line in a speech by a councillor at the Kilkenny meeting.

Then there was Father Michael Cleary's column – it's headed 'Dublin can be Heaven' in the *Dublin Tribune*. He wrote:

> "Politicians and media personnel who have condoned and accepted promiscuity, adultery, the commercialising of Sundays, information on abortion and who would put condoms freely into the hands of young people have spent the last week condemning Brian Lenihan's lie in more pious and sonorous terms than the whole Irish hierarchy could ever manage."

Father Cleary said he wasn't defending Brian Lenihan but:

> "...whether this lie wrecks Brian Lenihan's career or not, I will
> offer him the consolation that he can walk into any confession
> box and his transgression will only merit him three Hail Marys...
> Wasn't St Peter lucky he had only to deal with Christ? He told a
> very blatant lie and repeated it twice and yet he reached the top
> and became first president of Christ's Church."

Father Cleary's conclusion is that "morality has been pushed aside;
anti-social behaviour is a new criterion of sin". Which is new to me,
though I cannot say that I have kept up to date in these matters. But
there's a familiar ring to the notion that a lie is only a sin if you're up
to something in bed.

In the Senate, too, there were contributors to the debate. When
David Norris attempted to raise the question of the law on
homosexuality – on which the European Court of Human Rights has
delivered judgement – Dr Sean McCarthy of Fianna Fáil called across
to him: "You should consult your presidential colleague who is hot on
homosexuality and who might support your cause." And when Mr
Norris said he was used to being insulted and abused in the house, Dr
McCarthy replied: "I would never abuse Senator Norris, I can assure
you of that." (The Progressive Democrat members at least had the
gumption to dissociate themselves from the remark.)

An organisation styling itself Clann na bFinini meanwhile has
issued a leaflet accusing Ms Robinson of being anti-family and having
no respect for "our sacred Constitution" and Mr Currie of being a
strong advocate of divorce. Its slogan is: "*Do chum glóire Dé agus onóra
na hÉireann.*"

The depressing point about all of this, but about the political
statements in particular, is that we are being expected to take the
argument seriously in the context of the presidency and our view of
ourselves. We are being sold the idea that cutting corners and adopting

an *à la carte* approach to the institutions of the State are, in a manner of speaking, second nature to us. Or, if you take the view that we can't all be corrupt, that concern at morality in public affairs is confined to a few fuddy-duddies somewhere around South County Dublin. Morality stops on the Naas Road and the rest of the country is populated by furtive little lads, who spend their lives dodging around corners, with nervous tics induced by winking and nodding while they yelp: "Up the Republic."

This kind of stuff is an insult to the integrity of great swathes of the Irish people: to a majority of them in fact. It is an insult to the intelligence of all. (I met an oddity this week: an honest Mayo man.) The thing is absurd.

But then it's easy to forget that the same line was peddled successfully in the past. Garret the Good and Honest Jack were terms of derision. And the nonsense that all politicians are equally deceitful, hypocritical or filled with humbug is another convenient cover. If it was true, it would beg another question with unflattering implications: Why is it that it's the Fianna Fáil politicians who almost invariably get caught?

I would like to think that, on this occasion, they will get the answer: it isn't good enough.

A woman breaches our Berlin Wall

O NE OF OUR most enduring barriers came down this week, a year to the day since the fall of the Berlin Wall. To compare these happenings, as Mary Robinson did last night, is not as far-fetched as it seems. It helps explain why it is so heartening to see her now beside a newly breached image of ourselves and hear the message: Women First.

The comparison between the Wall and the barrier which Irish society constructed for itself – in terms of power, between the exclusive and the excluded – is worth pursuing. The Wall, you may remember, was not a towering structure, though it was fiercely guarded and anyone who approached it without official approval had to face a stretch of land sown only with mines and wire.

On closer inspection, however, it turned out to be shoddily built, covered in graffiti, and surrounded mostly by dank, uneasy streets. It was not so much fearsome as squalid; and the people who lived around it seemed to shrug it off as an ugly, if potentially lethal, fact of life.

It preserved an order of sorts, stubborn, grey and fearful; and it protected orators and their tinny rhetoric from the air of reality. When it finally came down, it was clear that the things it was meant to protect were already riddled to the core.

The Irish barrier which the election of Ms Robinson has so joyfully breached was, in its own way, grey and smug and squalid, too. It was less fearsomely protected than the Berlin Wall; but the legal, political and psychological structures that it buttressed were no less real or pervasive for being more democratic and less intimidating than the apparatus of which the Stasi was part.

When post-colonial Ireland cast about it for enemies to replace the old one which had departed with the garrison, when it sought an internal focus for its vengeance or an excuse for its own failure to live

41

up to expectations, it fastened on, among other things, a version of morality which saw sex as the only sin and women as the most provocative temptation.

An alliance of conservative politicians and determined bishops was convenient, though to give it the now popular title of a Rainbow Coalition would hardly be accurate. Rainbow it was not. But there was a certain symmetry about two clubs of elderly men, one of which was prepared to legislate for women as chattel, while the other consigned her to a form of second-class citizenship within the Roman Catholic Church. Both lived happily (and too long) with the contradiction that they were steeped in Mariolatry.

The practical results for women were punitive in the extreme; they were robbed of independence and dignity and smothered with guilt; fed on a pretence of importance and a place in society which would have them forever cabined and confined.

What made the presidential election such a vital and eventually such a gripping contest was the way in which it finally became a choice between Mary Robinson's conviction that, now at last, the Wall must fall, and Fianna Fáil's view that the less disturbance there was, the better; between an all-embracing coalition and a party which has carried its determination to stand alone to the verge of self-destruction.

I fear that many of the politicians now analysing what has happened are trying, not so much to understand the contest, as to explain it away. It was a contest between visions, one of which was undeniably conservative, while the other refused to be ideologically labelled, but stood broadly for change and specifically for a more vivid sense of the rights of minorities, of the need for social justice and of the long, unfinished march of women towards equality.

In the analyses of the politician, words and phrases are jumbled together in the hope that sooner or later, somehow or other, everything will fall into place and the jigsaw puzzle will be solved. So we hear about the urban versus rural thing, the woman's vote, protests by the young and the middle class; and we hear of a coalition of many colours. All of the jumbled words and phrases are intended to convey the impression that this was no ordinary part of our political culture; that it is a phenomenon unlikely to be repeated. Once-off, an accident, a freak.

This is nonsense and simply shows how the speakers have closed their eyes to the people around them, probably in the hope that the people around them are equally blind. This is not a criticism of Fianna Fáil and Fine Gael, not of the politicians of the left: Dick Spring, who chose Ms Robinson as candidate, or Proinsias de Rossa, who supported Mr Spring's inspired choice. Nor is it a criticism of the Progressive Democrats, who, despite their decision not to endorse Ms Robinson publicly, managed to express their admiration for her pretty clearly at a respectful distance.

Ms Robinson's camp had set out expecting (and at first would probably have been satisfied with) the combined votes of a coalition embracing Labour, the Workers' Party, the Greens and an independent or two; roughly 20 per cent, with perhaps a bonus of five or six percentage points from an electorate mistrustful of partisan politics; another four or five points from women who, in other circumstances, might have backed Fianna Fáil or Fine Gael.

Ms Robinson's band of romantic realists, however, soon recognised that taking a cool, clear look at the realities of Irish life was, surprisingly, more promising than living lazily with many of the commonplace assumptions. They recognised, for instance, that the urban–rural divide is not what it used to be. Ms Robinson's victory may have been fashioned in Dublin; but it could not have happened had her appeal – her mandate for change – not been made to Allihies and Ballylanders and Ballinamuck as well as to Dún Laoghaire.

They not only saw through the usual left-wing mistake of limiting a party's appeal to those fitting a very narrow description of working class, but the notion prevalent in sections of Fine Gael and most of Fianna Fáil that concern for ethics or social justice or modernisation is confined to a single postal district in Dublin where no real Irish person ever lived.

It's ironical – if not downright perverse – that parties which have worked hard to create a prosperous middle class capable of educating itself should fail to recognise the extent to which the class has grown and how its demands have become more sophisticated and less hidebound. It's odd that people who work daily with women, who may have been married or have close female relations, can't identify – and detect the direction of – a woman's vote, though some of them would probably refuse to recognise its validity anyway. (I am reminded here of a loud-mouthed acquaintance who refused to see merit in change of any sort and voted accordingly; his wife promptly neutralised his efforts by going out and voting in the opposite direction, but, sadly, democracy was her only retaliation.)

There are other ironies and contradictions in the reactions of Fianna Fáil and Fine Gael people to their defeat. The Fine Gael organisers, for example, will find, if they look closely enough, that the candidature of Mary Robinson took on the social-democratic character that Alan Dukes had proposed for the party when he took over from Garret FitzGerald in 1987.

Mr Dukes wasn't taken seriously and may not have been sufficiently convinced by his own proposal to impose it with a firm hand. In any event, some members of this parliamentary group preferred the party's old character – countrified, amateurish, conservative – while others found it hard to come to grips with the Tallaght Strategy. Both groups now blame Mr Dukes for the party's poor showing in the polls and specifically for the delay in nominating Austin Currie – a delay for which Mr Currie, an excellent candidate, paid heavily.

The Fine Gael front bench and parliamentary party might well take a look at its own performance – and at its reluctance to find a place in the spectrum of Irish politics and then stick to it. Otherwise, it will find itself with the functioning capacity the party demonstrated in an election not 20 years ago when, on a holiday weekend shortly before polling day, the entire headquarter's staff and leadership cadre shut up shop and took to the hills.

In Fianna Fáil's case, the refusal to look Irish society straight in the face is an older habit and one that will obviously be more difficult to correct. Even now, as its members recite a litany of praise for the performance of the Government elected 15 months ago, Fianna Fáil members shy away from the mention of coalition; talk wistfully of the day when the party can govern on its own and rarely, if ever, mention the Progressive Democrats – except, as in Brian Lenihan's case, to suggest that something nasty happened because of them.

Mr Lenihan may now feel that fortune, which had favoured him so often in the past, has finally deserted his side. Had Fianna Fáil held power on its own, had it not been in coalition with the Progressive Democrats, the party might have weathered the storm that blew up over the contradictions and denials of the last couple of weeks. On several occasions over the years, when the evidence against it was nearly, but not quite, as strong, stonewalling had done the trick.

Unconvincing leadership and poor tactical advice added to the Lenihan camp's misfortune in the presidential race. The Progressive Democrats' willingness to risk an election on the question of principle was seriously misjudged. The impact of the candidate's televised confrontation, not with an opponent, but with himself as accuser, was so strong that it could neither be dodged nor forgotten.

And it wasn't just Mr Lenihan, but a chorus of his front-bench colleagues – Charles Haughey, Pádraig Flynn, Ray Burke and Bertie Ahern – who stood exposed as if paralysed by their own bad luck, bad judgement and bad performance. When it was all over, they looked everywhere for scapegoats – except where the real culprits sit.

Time for parties to listen to hard chaws

NOW IS THE time for the hard chaws to come to the aid of their parties. These are the people who sift through election results like forensic teams examining bomb debris. Skill and instinct help them discover what's happened; sense and experience should tell them why.

What sets them apart from the rest of party loyalists is that they steadfastly refuse to let their convictions colour their judgement. This may not make them the most loved members of their parties; it should lend invaluable weight to their findings.

That, of course, is only the beginning. Getting the party bosses to take any notice of the finding is another day's work. During a campaign, politicians are apt to be caught up in the mood their managers have paid to create. In extreme cases, the condition outlasts the campaign and the politicians fall prey to delusions – specifically, they begin to believe their own propaganda.

There is nothing more saddening, then, than to meet a fully grown political leader, with a glassy smile on his face as he murmurs: "They love me, you know. They really do." It is to prevent such toad-like flights from reality that the hard chaws are called in. The audience that so loved him, they explain as gently as possible, was his own hand-picked and well-primed crowd. If he'd proposed a bout of anaconda wrestling on the Amazon, their reactions would have been the same: they are there to applaud, not listen.

On the other hand, there are graphs and charts, opinion polls and tallymen's notes, first and second counts, which tell a different story. Now, if only the party bosses could learn from these, the party might do better next time round.

Fine Gael's parliamentary group did not wait for the hard chaws to do their stuff. The move against Alan Dukes had begun before counting was completed. He had resigned before the evidence was fully assembled. The mood in the party was like that of the forces in the Williamite wars who cried, "Change leaders and we'll fight you again." What Fine Gael needed, it seemed, was a simple answer to a complex question.

Some of the prime movers against Mr Dukes had never taken to his social-democratic ways; indeed, they'd been unhappy with Garret FitzGerald's constitutional crusade, which they blamed for the Fine Gael–Labour coalition's loss of popularity in the 1980s. When, at their last ardfheis, Mr Dukes called for a renewal of the philosophy that had inspired the 'Just Society' programme of the 1960s, they took the hint of a modest step to the left as the final straw.

True, Mr Dukes had contributed some unforced errors towards the movement which led to this fall, causing some of his erstwhile allies on the social-democratic front to join his critics. But those who now announce that, in choosing John Bruton, they have made a change for the better must prove their point. Mr Bruton may turn out to be a better organised and more popular leader, but will Fine Gael become, in the long run, a party more attuned to the demands of the 1990s?

Even in its social-democratic heyday, when it looked as though it might become the biggest party in the State, Fine Gael fell into a trap that had already snared and, in a sense paralysed, Fianna Fáil. Fine Gael's head may have been inclined towards social democracy, but its heart wanted to be all things to as many segments of the electorate as possible.

Reluctant to abandon its old constituency and afraid of embracing too wholeheartedly the new, it adopted a form of pragmatism which eventually proved unattractive to both. Fianna Fáil is better off only to the extent that it holds a bigger share of the popular vote. If Fine Gael has been beaten into third place for the first time in a national contest, Fianna Fáil has failed to achieve its ambition in the sixth election in a row.

And if Fine Gael has yet to decide where its future lies, Fianna Fáil has refused to recognise the need for such a decision. Charles Haughey has asked his colleagues to consider why the party consistently starts election campaigns with a substantial lead and ends up failing to reach its goal.

Some in the party suggest that only a few percentage points separate Fianna Fáil from victory. All they really need is one more push. If only they could redouble their efforts... and so on.

But how many times has Fianna Fáil to suffer the frustration of electoral failure (in its terms) before calling in the hard chaws to have a look at the party and its appeal and to measure both against the electorate and its demands?

Fine Gael appears to have decided against social democracy in the aftermath of a campaign which ended with a resounding victory for the social-democratic candidate. It was a victory achieved without the financial or organisational resources of its opponents; victory for a vision of society which may not be socialist but is nonetheless forward looking and unafraid of change.

Fianna Fáil's response during the campaign was to retreat into the old fundamentalist haunts which have served it poorly in five general elections. It complained of the Rainbow Coalition ranged against it (a coalition which included its partners in Government, the Progressive Democrats) while ignoring the fact that throughout the campaign – as in every general election since its foundation – the party had refused to contemplate an alliance with anyone else.

Fianna Fáil appears to imagine a constituency out there, in the midlands or beyond the Shannon, populated by nationalists who want more of the past, not hope for the future. But the constituency is shrinking and, in any event, is less receptive to the old messages than it used to be.

In the first of the two constitutional referendums in the 1980s, five Dublin constituencies went against the conservative grain. In the second referendum, there were six. In the presidential election, the Dublin and Munster regions emphatically supported Mary Robinson;

and even in Connacht–Ulster she took three Dáil areas, two of them in her home county, Mayo.

The myth that the State continues to be firmly and irrevocably divided between a metropolitan minority and a majority of truly national, truly orthodox country folk has been exploded. If the leaders of Fianna Fáil, or for that matter Fine Gael, imagine that they can depend on the midlands, parts of the West and the border counties to sustain them, their hard chaws with the graphs, charts and poll results must be falling down on the job.

Speculation about the modernisation of Irish politics has followed every election here since the early 1980s. Europeanisation, you may recall, was the catchword in 1987 and 1989. Everyone agreed about the volatility of the electorate.

We've been listening to talk about the young vote since 1977. The opening up of Irish society as a result of greater contact with the world outside has become a cliché. The only people who haven't caught up with the societal changes which caused the volatility and undermined the assumptions of Irish politics are the two main parties with their catch-all appeal.

JANUARY 19th, 1991

Finding our place in the global village

THE WEEK FINDS us in a time warp – caught between the first war to have been fought as a television spectacle and a dilemma inherited from Éamon de Valera.

The bombing raids on Baghdad started on cue, in time for the evening news on the American networks. The CNN crews in the city became, even before the pilots in the planes overhead, its first heroes.

Prime time that night was reserved for President George Bush's address to the nation, its euphoric reception setting the tone for the round-the-clock coverage that was to follow, with the ever-present CNN crews in the lead.

With a bewildering armoury of high technology to command, they were first with the action as and where it happened, in Baghdad, Dhahran, Jerusalem; first too with interpretation, opinion and surmise, from the White House, Capitol Hill and the Pentagon.

The other participants in the multinational force were partners in a coalition acting on foot of the United Nations' resolutions. But this was, in a real sense, America's war. The United States, in military matters and in the supply of information, was calling the shots.

The tracer bullets in the sky over Baghdad reminded the CNN men of the Fourth of July. Less endowed media please copy.

Now that it's becoming more familiar, there is time to examine the language of the commentary. It's made to match the impression that it's intended to convey. The talk is of surgical strikes and pinpoint accuracy, targets taken out and missions accomplished.

If it has a familiar ring in the ears of the young audiences from Bangkok to Ballyhaunis, it's not because they can remember Vietnam where much of the lingo was invented. That was too long ago.

No, these are echoes from that other world where life is simple, Superman goes "pow" and Lex Luther gets his deserts. In such a world, strikes are always surgical and death is the ultimate unreality. There are no blood casualties and there are no mixed feelings.

The congressman interviewed after the US Senate had given the President a blank cheque on Thursday evening caught the mood: "One President, one nation, one Senate, one destiny."

So did his colleague, who called the anti-war protestors outside the White House "excuses for men". There has never been any shortage of people ready to hand out white feathers, at a safe distance.

Nor is there any shortage of young men who will fight because they have nothing better to do or bewildered families who are nudged in the direction of patriotism – "How d'you feel when you listen to the President?" – but simply want it all over and done with.

But life is far from simple; and, of course, there are mixed feelings, even in time of war. It is not a case of one side being as bad as the other: I would take my chances any day with George Bush in preference to Saddam Hussein.

Even to complain about Mr Bush's way of going about his business (and ours, for he's doing it in the name of the United Nations) is to acknowledge the difference. In the US, the right to complain exists. To think of Mr Saddam Hussein's way is to remember the *Observer* journalist, Farzad Bazoft, dangling on a rope.

Of course, the Americans are open to criticisms of inconsistency and hypocrisy and, of course, there is a dilemma for those who like to share their way of life but would prefer to have nothing to do with the means by which they choose to protect it.

And the dilemma is particularly acute for a state with an open and vulnerable economy and a foreign policy of which neutrality is considered the cornerstone; a state which rejected dependence on a powerful neighbour to become independent but has yet to find its way in a world where interdependence is the key to collective security.

The debate in the Dáil yesterday was provoked by the war in the Gulf. But, more than that, it was about our place in the international community; and the decision to provide facilities for the US at Shannon clearly suggested where that place might be.

It confronted a dilemma about neutrality which de Valera had faced – and resolved by making the policy conditional before the ink was dry on the document. In his case, public neutrality was combined with covert support for the allies in the Second World War.

And, as the recently released State papers showed, when membership of the UN was first considered, there was still further agonising over whether or not the obligations of membership were consistent with neutrality.

The problem was back with the Dáil yesterday in a debate which ended with the parties of the left convinced that the policy – never precisely defined – had finally been abandoned; specifically by Fine Gael and the Progressive Democrats, less openly by the Taoiseach.

As Mr Gerard Collins put it: "There can be no question of involving neutrality in connection with our obligations under the UN Charter. All members of the UN, regardless of their declared status, agree to be bound by the Charter."

Mr Des O'Malley was even more pointed: "This is not an issue on which we are, or ought to be, neutral. There can be no neutrality on the question of backing the United Nations and its resolutions and – in turn – their implications in the context of Saddam Hussein's invasion of Kuwait."

Although some of yesterday's protagonists may not care to admit it, we seem to have found our place in the global village.

MARCH 9th, 1991

A curious case of condoms and change

I WENT TO bed happy on Wednesday night and woke up in the 1950s. There, on the front page of Thursday's *Irish Times*, was Dr Desmond Connell's announcement that he was planning to follow the example set by Dr Cahal Daly and campaign against contraception.

On the radio, too, someone was slowly circling his subject like a man who couldn't bring himself to pick up something distasteful. A voice with a wince in it spoke of "these things", "those objects" and with a sudden rush of frankness "these so-called prophylactics".

It turned out to be Dr Vincent Twomey, lecturer in moral theology at St Patrick's College, Maynooth, talking about condoms.

On Wednesday, he had written in this paper on the same subject and in equally roundabout terms, like a Fianna Fáil Minister at the RDS talking about coalition – or Brian Lenihan's dismissal.

Dr Twomey's interest was excited by a leading article on the Circuit Court case in which the Irish Family Planning Association had been fined for selling a condom to a garda in the Virgin Megastore. Dr Connell's announcement was a comment on Charles Haughey's reaction to the predictable mirth the case provoked at home and abroad.

The Taoiseach told the parliamentary party that the Government was proposing to change the law under which the action had been taken. Condoms would be made more widely available without prescription; and the age at which people might buy them would be lowered from 18 to 16, the age at which they may marry.

To some it might have seemed a modest proposal – capable no doubt of being hedged round with conditions that would make it resemble the original Irish solution. To the majority of Fianna Fáil TDs and senators, it came as a bolt from the blue. They were by all accounts shocked into silence.

Many of them, after all, are old enough to remember the tragicomic history of Irish politicians' attempts to get to grips with the issue since Liam Cosgrave's historic quickstep across the floor of the Dáil to help defeat the Bill of his own Minister, Pat Cooney, on a free vote in the 1970s.

Most of them must recall how, just over six years ago, Des O'Malley was expelled from Fianna Fáil for conduct unbecoming a member of the party. What he had done was to abstain on Barry Desmond's amendment of Mr Haughey's notorious solution. The speech he made was to become one of the rallying cries of the Progressive Democrats: "I stand by the Republic."

And they hardly needed Dr Connell to remind them how Fianna Fáil had formed an alliance with the Roman Catholic Church to wreck

Garret FitzGerald's constitutional crusade in the referendums on divorce and abortion in the 1980s. For the Church has always needed a party to do its bidding as the archbishop tacitly acknowledged on Wednesday night.

It was, he said:

> "Extraordinary that no political party in the country is prepared to defend what so many people regard as fundamental values of family life... Truly extraordinary that so many of our people are to be effectively disenfranchised by such measures. Of course, it is a matter for the people themselves ultimately."

It is indeed. But the complaint itself was as extraordinary as the suggestion of disenfranchisement, which of course is nonsense. It was as if Dr Connell sensed the beginning of the end of the relationship between Church and State which has had such a profound influence on Irish life for almost 70 years.

But the Fianna Fáil politicians who chose to talk about it later, with a couple of exceptions, gave the opinions of Dr Daly and Dr Connell short shrift. In an astonishing display of pragmatism, they took the view that Church leaders ought to be heard but not necessarily obeyed on social issues.

This may not, after all, prove to be the 1950s revisited. But, even as we speculate on the reasons for Mr Haughey's Pauline conversion, it is necessary to be cautious. Mr Des Hanafin, one of those resistant to change, claims that both Mr Haughey and Rory O'Hanlon feel distinctly uncomfortable about the Government's proposal.

Dr O'Hanlon certainly refrained from providing specific details to the Senate on Wednesday night and his silence may be significant. As for Mr Haughey, contrary to Mr Hanafin's opinion, his friends say he is about to surprise everyone by proving himself, in a manner of speaking, gung ho for social progress.

If so, we may well ask what has wrought the change? Has the message of Mrs Mary Robinson's splendid victory at last been driven home? Are the Progressive Democrats yet again exerting a benign influence disproportionate to their strength? Have Fianna Fáil's own home-grown progressives like Charlie McCreevy, Micheál Martin and Tom Kitt, finally succeeded in rousing their Rip Van Winkle?

Who knows better than the organisers of Fianna Fáil how shrewdly the bishops and their fundamentalist prompters may marshal – and manipulate – the sociological arguments against change of almost any kind when it comes to legislation governing sexual activity?

There may be – though I hesitate to suggest it for fear of disturbing any hope of progress – a less noble reason for change than any of those listed above. Condoms will not be the only, and may not be the trickiest, issue on the minds of delegates at the ardfheis this weekend. The party's leaders are in a tight corner; and the Lenihan case is only the most embarrassing of the problems.

Last year, the debate on organisation produced polite but serious criticism of the way the foot soldiers were being led – and left out of the party's decision making. They voted for a commission, essentially to examine their grievances. It was promised again after the disaster of the presidential election and was eventually set up after a further delay of several months. So far, it is said to have met on only three occasions.

Now, to judge by the resolutions on organisation, there is urgent pressure for results. About 15 resolutions deal with the commission itself, several others call for action which would effectively democratise the party; the organisers are asked to emphasise the roles of women, young people and the rank and file; there are calls for better communications between different levels of the party.

Many of the resolutions are no different from those which appeared in the agenda last year. And that tells a story which will not be overshadowed by the question of condoms when the delegates have their say tomorrow morning. We may yet be in for a lively weekend.

Fewer ostriches and more eagles, please

PADDY SMITH OF RTÉ announced lately that ostrich farming had begun in England; and he wondered if it might take on here. I was surprised he hadn't noticed: we've been growing our own for years.

Not, I may add, without success. A foreign correspondent who was here for the general election asked why it was that candidates in Ireland invariably *stood* for office while in the United States and Britain they *ran* for it. The answer of course is that you can't run for anything with your head in the sand; and some of our home-grown ostriches have made it to the top while maintaining this well-known national position.

Nor are our ostriches confined to politics. Some have taken the cloth and are in the hierarchy. Others are well to the fore in the trade-union movement. A few have found their way into the higher echelons of the ESB. What all of them have in common with some of our political leaders is a reluctance to confront reality until disaster is staring them in the face.

The Progressive Democrats, who are meeting in Cork this weekend, have made confronting reality their stock in trade; and they have managed to do it more successfully than many of their critics would allow or the electorate by and large is prepared to acknowledge. Whether they have also succeeded in meeting the standards of their most demanding activists is something the weekend will tell.

The conference will be the first of three stern tests for the party. The second will be the local elections in June, when they must win a substantial block of seats if they are to establish a badly needed national network. The third will be the first review of the Coalition's performance in July after two years in office.

The fact that it is a coalition seems to have escaped the attention of some commentators, who are as unwilling to lift their heads from the sand as many of the politicians they admire. It is a popular illusion. Most people, steeped in a political culture which sees single-party government as good government, think only of Fine Gael–Labour partnerships when coalition is mentioned. Yet there has only been one single-party majority government since 1973 and to say that it was not a success would be an understatement.

Getting Fianna Fáil into coalition in the first place was one of the Progressive Democrats' achievements which ought not to be forgotten. It marked a turning point in politics, as significant in its way as the presidential election, though for different reasons.

At the Labour Party conference in Killarney, Barry Desmond said that the State would have coalition governments for the next 25 years; and he was right. Charles Haughey is said to have acknowledged as much when he reminded colleagues that, given the new circumstances, Fianna Fáil could be in government for as long as it chose. (That is to say, for as long as it could find parties to partner it.)

Getting Fianna Fáil into coalition was one thing: getting popular recognition for the nature of coalition is another. Labour leaders must have been sick, sore and weary reading about their party's dilemma when they shared power with Fine Gael and Fine Gael was used to partnership. Fianna Fáil is not; and there are bound to be headlines this weekend about the dilemma and the identity problem of the Progressive Democrats.

And if the Progressive Democrats attempt to resolve their "dilemma" by asserting their identity, the instant ostrich-like reaction will be to squawk "split"! Never mind that, for decades, parties all over Europe have entered partnerships on the basis of agreed programmes and renegotiated partnerships when they weren't being fulfilled; in Ireland, coalition, like marriage, is forever and weaker partners that make their beds are expected to lie on them in silent endurance.

The Progressive Democrats have had some of their policies accepted by Fianna Fáil, which is to the credit of both parties. There is at long last a Companies Act which should help to counteract some corporate abuse. A badly needed Competition Bill has been published and is being debated. An environmental protection agency is on the way.

The party has had a degree of influence on the Government's more conciliatory attitude to the North, specifically its welcome support for Peter Brooke's courageous initiative. Des O'Malley's speech on Articles 2 and 3 of the Constitution was generally agreed to have been among the most convincing arguments for change in a historic debate.

But on several of its own most cherished policies, the party has had little or no success. The promised reform of the Oireachtas is 15 months overdue. Reform of local government is proceeding at a snail's pace and, in any event, looks like being fudged. Tax cuts, some of them quite illusory, are used to dodge the promise of radical reform.

On the question of condoms, the Progressive Democrats have found themselves as divided as their partners but with this significant difference: Fianna Fáil has only lately arrived – well, almost arrived – at a liberal position on social issues; it was part of the Progressive Democrats' stock in trade, of its programme to confront reality.

Can the Progressive Democrats be satisfied with the lack of debate on privitisation and the failure to answer questions raised here and elsewhere about the procedure followed in the Greencore case and likely to be followed in the case of Irish Life?

The Progressive Democrats have an unambiguous approach to political, economic and monetary union in the European Community. Can they not persuade their partners to provide the information which the public clearly believes it lacks?

The Progressive Democrats lay claim to openness and in opposition contributed to the debate on the Goodman affair. We have not yet heard how export credit insurance was made available to that group in 1987, by whom and at whose request. Can the Progressive Democrats be satisfied with the handling of Patrick Gallagher's banking activities? Or with the disposal of Carysfort Training College, which was bought by UCD in circumstances that have not been fully explained?

When Mr O'Malley took action to stop the preferential treatment of which the Goodman group had availed, there were many expressions of relief, some from parties which, in other respects, would have been at least as critical of the Progressive Democrats as of their partners. Had the Progressive Democrats not been in government, they said, had the Government not been a coalition, the State would have been at risk of substantial losses.

In the June elections, the Progressive Democrat programme will reflect the slogan of this weekend's conference. It reads: "Clean Up Local Government". It is a reminder that among the reasons for their existence – indeed for their participation in government – is the belief that national as well as local affairs need fewer ostriches and sharper vigilance.

JULY 27th, 1991

Land of contrast where the old ways are best

WE NOW HAVE a Dáil committee on crime. Its chairwoman, Mairin Quill, says that juvenile delinquency and "an explosion of teenage crime" will be at the top of its agenda. We do not have a forum on unemployment.

The Government has started to fiddle with problems presented by this year's budgetary miscalculations. But Albert Reynolds says that plans for next year's Budget will be discussed as usual by the Cabinet and announced in the usual way. We do not have a finance committee and it's unlikely the Estimates will be discussed before most of the money has been spent.

Some of the providers of health services are worried about a lack of funds this year and expect to be better off next year. The best they can hope for, by dint of scrimping and stalling, is to be able to muddle through. And they fear that improvements promised in the Programme for Economic and Social Progress may soon be quietly forgotten. They have been offered no reassurance.

I have chosen these items from the news of the past fortnight to make this point: it is not that there are decent things the Government would like to do, but can't; rather, that there are sensible things it can do – but won't.

Setting up a committee on crime is a good idea which doesn't need to be justified. Indeed, Ms Quill accepts that, among other things, it must investigate the social factors leading to that explosion: one-third of the recorded car-stealing, handbag-snatching and house-breaking is carried out by teenagers.

Pat McCartan of the Workers' Party agrees with Ms Quill about the social factors, but not with the description of the explosion. He wants the Whitaker Report to be the committee's guide. You can be forgiven for not remembering the Whitaker Report. No one else does. It favoured penal reform and was generally welcomed by those involved with prisoners and the prison service. It was published in 1985. It hasn't been heard of since.

Other members of the crime committee favour a more direct approach. Ben Briscoe of Fianna Fáil doesn't want it to become a talking shop. He says it should concentrate on providing secure detention centres for young offenders. Sean Barrett of Fine Gael complains that the absence of custodial places creates an impression that young people can continue in a life of crime because there is no place to put them.

In this familiar argument, I suspect, the Barrett–Briscoe line will prevail. Even if it doesn't, this is clearly a case of putting the cart before the horse. Crime was considered a serious problem in 1985. It still is. But to establish a committee to discuss it while refusing to set up a forum on unemployment is, in the most insulting sense, all too Irish.

Those politicians who pay more than passing attention to social problems occasionally look at our level of unemployment and poverty – the worst and second worst in the European Community – and wonder privately why there has not been trouble on the streets. But there is trouble on the streets, as Ms Quill knows; the fact that it takes the form of "an explosion of teenage crimes" doesn't make it any less threatening or less likely to grow.

Most politicians, however, don't care to look too closely at social problems. Like Mr Barrett and Mr Briscoe, they prefer the direct, uncomplicated approach to law and order. Theirs is a world of dangerous simplicity in which you can't improve on the traditional response.

Mr Reynolds thinks so, too. He refuses to recognise that, if there had been a committee to monitor the State's finances, their deterioration would not have been sprung on an unsuspecting public – and, to all appearances, on a gormless Government – in the middle of the year.

An entire committee could hardly have missed the Gulf War or the recessions in Britain and the United States, as Mr Reynolds obviously did. One or two of its members might have spotted that unemployment was on the way up.

The war was at its height and the recessions were well under way when the Budget was written and the Programme for Economic and Social Progress agreed. Last weekend, on RTÉ Radio's *This Week*, Mr Reynolds was still insisting that they took his strategists by surprise. But even as he struggles with this year's miscalculations, and after the rows about the miserably inadequate debate on the Estimates, the thought never crosses his mind that the business of arriving at the 1992 Budget might benefit from the tiniest improvements.

It is not as if all that needed attention now, as a result of the current muddle, was a slight adjustment in book-keeping. People's lives and the services they depend on are affected.

Rory O'Hanlon must have reported already that the Western Health Board is thinking of suing his department for more than £9.8 million in overdue grants. The board is holding almost £2.55 million in cheques which it is unable to pay. It has reached the limit of its £3.5 million overdraft. Its chief executive, Eamon Hannan, quoted by the *Western People*, says that there are:

> "...no more rabbits in the hat: the only way we can cut back is to eliminate services. I can't see myself making such a recommendation to the board. Services are at the minimum."

But Mr Hannan and his colleagues are expected to go on pulling rabbits out of empty hats while a speculative report in *The Irish Times* a week ago about the likely postponement of some of the PESP's most important social elements has gone without denial.

The politicians, like the health boards, will muddle on into 1992 without a foreign affairs committee, without a finance committee and without a forum on unemployment – but with a committee on crime.

We have, of course, a few other attractions to offer the discerning visitor. The K Club at Straffan House, for instance, about which Frank McDonald wrote: "Ireland has never seen anything like it. It is as if a piece of West Palm Beach had been planted in Co. Kildare."

Michael Smurfit and the directors of Amisfield invested £27 million in the K Club (once the home of Patrick Gallagher, the banker now detained in a Belfast jail). Life membership went up from £100,000 to £125,000 because the initial offer was oversubscribed. The dearest bedroom suite in the place costs £700 a night, the cheapest single room £125.

Charles Haughey, who went down there for the opening last week, said that it was "a courageous and far-seeing venture targeted at satisfying the need for a world-class small hotel and country club", something to "further the profile of what Ireland has to offer abroad".

You'll be glad to know that our leader didn't go empty-handed. As a small token of appreciation, the Department of Finance contributed £608,643 out of the European Regional Development Fund to the K Club. The equivalent of a mere six life memberships, at the cheap rate. Or one-quarter of the amount the Western Health Board can't afford to pay out. It is, as the woman said, a funny old world.

NOVEMBER 9th, 1991

Gerry Collins' vintage performance sets them rolling in the aisles

GERARD COLLINS OBVIOUSLY subscribes to an old political motto: when in doubt dither and, if that doesn't work, take a deep breath, count to three – and panic.

His performance on RTÉ's *Six-One News* on Thursday night was the highlight of the week, against stiff competition: Albert Reynolds and Pádraig Flynn sacked; Fianna Fáil and the Government lurching from uncertainty towards crisis; Charles Haughey complaining of a power-grab and Mr Reynolds of instability.

Much of this had yet to happen on Thursday night. But Mr Collins was stricken. "I believe," said he, "that what Albert is doing now is wrong, that he should, even at this late stage, pull back from wrecking the Government and throwing the country into panic and chaos."

If the country was not already in panic and chaos, it must have been starting to feel that way. Mr Collins certainly was. "And I for my part," said he, "am supporting my Taoiseach. I trust him. I respect his authority. His office. And the dignity of that office."

Sean Duignan's eyebrow was beginning to develop a sympathetic twitch. Mr Collins, however, wasn't addressing him and may not even have been talking to the audience, which by now was rolling in the aisles, perhaps in panic and chaos; certainly in convulsions.

Gerry (we are on first-name terms here) had his eye on Albert. And Albert had just stolen a march on Gerry by nipping in to support Sean Power's "no confidence" motion, which made him first in the field for the leadership stakes.

"And might I say, Albert," said Gerry, "before you vote and before you issue this particular statement in the formal sense – Albert – face up to your responsibilities and, if you feel as solemnly as you believe you do, well you've no option but to give us your resignation even before you vote on Saturday."

And as he was led away, weeping into a big white handkerchief that he'd bought somewhere out foreign, he was replaced on the screen by Albert, who seemed remarkably unmoved by the outburst. He said his piece with the calm assurance that made you wish he'd had a place in the Government all along – as Minister for Finance maybe – while the rest of us were being plunged into the panic and chaos that had poor Mr Collins a-dither.

Instead, of course, Mr Reynolds had been a leader-in-waiting, paring his nails as Charles Haughey, with the help of P J Mara, waded deeper and deeper in the mud that he'd hoped might cover Dick Spring or, at any rate, make him look more like "one of our own".

But, by now, the old mudslinger and his sidekick were not shooting straight – and that was before Mr Power's motion hit the fan. Mr Spring said their efforts were dangerous and demented; and to anyone who watched *Oireachtas Report* on Wednesday night, it didn't sound like a word of a lie, which was more than could be said of the Haughey–Mara version of events.

First, Mr Spring was associated with the developer of the Telecom site, Pat Doherty. Then he wasn't; they'd met once, a long time ago at an embassy reception. Of course, there is nothing to it. All Mr Haughey and Mr Mara had been trying to do was to make the point that, if it had been Mr Haughey who had met Mr Doherty, all sorts of questions would have been raised.

Well, Mr Haughey had met the chairman of Greencore, Mr Bernie Cahill, and all sorts of questions were raised. Some had been transferred out of harm's way in the Dáil; as for the rest, it was proving hard to get answers – certainly answers that matched.

First Mr Haughey hadn't met Mr Cahill. Then he had, but it wasn't the kind of meeting that Mr Spring had suggested. They hadn't discussed the appointment of financial advisers. Well, they had, but there hadn't been pressure for the appointment of NCB. Everyone knew that Mr Cahill had said so; but everyone knew that Mr Cahill had not.

Now there was another accusation for Mr Spring to answer: that he'd been in league with Chris Comerford, had indeed made a phone call on his behalf to a trade unionist on the board of the company. But the trade unionist was dead and Mr Spring didn't know him or, for that matter, Mr Comerford; in any event the Labour leader was out of the country on holidays when the call was made.

All of this was doing two things. It reminded the watching public of the scandals that had set off the train of events that led to an erosion of confidence in the Government and Mr Haughey's problems. And it kept the attention of Fianna Fáil backbenchers and the Progressive Democrats on Mr Haughey's leadership.

For both parties, though for somewhat different reasons, matters were coming to a head. The Progressive Democrats' problem still persists and is rendered even more acute by the departure from

Government of Mr Reynolds and Mr Flynn and the criticisms made by their junior colleagues.

How could the party remain in a Government whose leader had lost the confidence of his Minister of Finance? Des O'Malley's typically cryptic message after a national executive meeting on Thursday night was that it would watch and wait for the outcome of today's Fianna Fáil meeting.

In Fianna Fáil, the difficulties run deeper. They arise from the kind of party it is and its reliance on the leadership. Mr Collins sensed the depth of the problem but would probably not acknowledge its origins, long term or immediate (not at least until the die had been cast, preferably by someone else).

Like all populist parties, Fianna Fáil sees its leader as a philosopher king. Considering itself a national movement, the party and the nation are one. In these circumstances, it scarcely needs either programmes or rules. Broad national aims are sufficient; pragmatism is elevated to the point of principle; and policies are what the leader says they are.

In fact, in all matters of importance, the leader's word goes, which is why Mr Collins became so excited when it was not only questioned but challenged – and by a Cabinet colleague too. To be guilty of disloyalty at this level is tantamount to treason.

This, you may have gathered, is not a modern political scheme of things. And some of the younger TDs who have spoken up in the past couple of days seem to recognise it.

When a populist movement – whether it's Peronism in Argentina or Gaullism in France or Fianna Fáil in this State – finds itself confronted by a modernising society with a set of new and complex demands, it also finds itself in a crisis which threatens its survival.

Fianna Fáil has changed, and changed radically, over the years: from entering the Dáil in 1927, adopting industrial programmes in the late 1950s, to forming a coalition in 1989. But only the first may have been as traumatic as its present condition. And this is made worse by the fact that, in the first instance, the current conflict is not about policy, but power – in a sense, not only the control, but the ownership of the party.

If and when power changes hands, a bigger task awaits it.

FEBRUARY 22nd, 1992

A week when old and new collide

IN TIME WE may come to see the week's events as another collision between the old Ireland and the new, a shameful episode in the struggle of the present to free itself from the clutches of the past.

How long will it take to heal the wounds inflicted on a 14-year-old and her family who find themselves trapped between the two? Readers of Franz Kafka who have been following their case must feel they are on familiar ground.

A young girl tells her parents of a crime committed against her; they go to the police. The State's senior officials are involved and the family is called back when, like thousands of others, it travels abroad for help.

Suddenly, with one of those sickening jolts which turns the world upside down, she is transformed from victim to defendant: confined like a prisoner to a State which officially recognises only one way out of her problem but unofficially admits that another way exists, if only she could take it.

But that leads beyond the boundaries of the State and, since her parents have brought her case to the notice of the authorities, she is no longer free to leave. It is as if she must stay to share the guilt for the crime committed against her.

And while we wait for the Supreme Court to hear the parents' appeal, and hope the wait will not be too long, contending voices are raised in this once airless room which we had once thought a republic.

Mary Robinson, who speaks more eloquently than anyone else for the new Ireland, recognises society's role in the affair when she says that, in this unhappy week, we are experiencing as a people a very deep crisis in ourselves. Her hope is that we may find the courage to face and resolve it.

Albert Reynolds, whose promise of an open and caring society was no sooner made than it was challenged by this crisis, accepts the President's statement as a reflection of popular compassion, but relies in the first instance on the Supreme Court to provide a solution.

But as Dr Conor Gearty, a senior lecturer in law at King's College, London, wrote in this paper on Thursday:

"The truth is that there are no human rights other than those that are won through political struggle and determined campaigning. Law is no substitute for politics.

"Judges can occasionally deliver short cuts on the way to freedom, but such advances are always contingent on political consolidation. It is no part of the judicial function to protect through deceit the false self-image of a hypocritical nation. The Irish people voted in this anti-abortion amendment..."

The amendment was indeed an effort by the old Ireland to steel itself against the new. It was prepared to ensure, at any price, that our legislators would be faced with the utmost difficulties if they ever decided, in response to the new, to amend or repeal the legal prohibition on abortion which had been effective for 120 years.

Political opportunism, cowardice and ineptitude played a part in having the crudest and most restrictive wording accepted. So did clerical intervention when Catholic leaders followed where their fundamentalist brethren led. Most joined with a will the campaign to portray opponents of the amendment as supporters of abortion.

The old Ireland relied – it still does – on formulae and slogans. It survived on abstractions and absolutes; on the obliteration from its consciousness of any human face.

The wording of the amendment was the price exacted on the women of the State. The nodding and winking which ignored the traffic to Britain – 5,000 abortions a year – was a *quid pro quo* for allowing the question of abortion to be considered closed; another Irish solution to an Irish problem.

It was reminiscent of the district courts of old when solicitors regularly pleaded for leniency on the grounds that the defendant had the ticket to Birmingham in his pocket: "Apply the Probation Act, your worship, and he won't trouble you again."

The medical, legal and ethical debates of the 1983 campaign occasionally sounded as if they had little enough to do with reality. The political foundation on which the ban was built was firmly rooted in hypocrisy.

The President speaks of the need for courage which we have not always had and the Taoiseach promises that no option must be considered closed, including that of a referendum. But courage will not be displayed by accepting that the Supreme Court's ruling is the last word on the matter, however impassioned the hope that it will resolve the immediate problem for the victim and her family.

A thicket of question marks has been raised – by politicians, lawyers, journalists, letter writers, contributors to radio programmes, in every public place. Anger and frustration are expressed. There is a sense of bewilderment: was this what the amendment really stood for and what those who voted for it intended?

Does the High Court's decision impinge on the right of citizens to travel to other European Community states and avail of services that are legally available there? Why should the Attorney General feel obliged to act in the public interest in this case but not, as counsel made clear, in the beef industry tribunal?

If the High Court's decision, with its prohibition on travel, stands, what are the implications for the "imprescriptible" constitutional rights of the family in this instance? Is it possible that similar restrictions will be placed on known or suspected terrorists whose missions are often lethal and always of doubtful legality? And so on.

The Government is seriously worried by the extent and tone of reporting abroad. Most foreign commentators are astonished, and in many cases appalled, to discover on the fringe of Europe a society whose blend of religion and politics comes close to that of the theocratic states where the writ of Islam runs.

Mr Reynolds has wisely called on the assistance of the opposition parties and the Progressive Democrats. They have a common interest: securing immediate relief for the victim. But they are not by any means agreed on what to do if, next week, relief is not forthcoming.

Opportunism, cowardice and ineptitude – the tendency to give way to religious pressure groups – has left politicians generally, but Fianna Fáil in particular, with a dreadful legacy. It can be overcome, if the habit of relying on the courts, the EC, or the short memories of the electorate is finally broken. The feeling that, once the immediate crisis has passed, a long-term solution can wait, has landed us in trouble once too often.

The Government will be criticised in some quarters, whatever it does. If legislation cannot be devised to protect the quality of women's lives as well as the unborn (in accordance with the Eighth Amendment), then the Constitution will have to be amended again.

It would not be easily done. But too much is at stake to worry about political difficulties or personal difficulties or personal inconveniences. Lives may be at risk – a claim which was dismissed as hysterical in 1983. Our national self-respect and international reputation must be restored. Politically there is a threat to the referendum on EC developments if attack comes from both conservative and liberal directions.

This will be a test of leadership and courage. The penalties for failure should not be underestimated; a government which lost the European issue, with or without the Maastricht Protocol, would have no option but to resign. How the Government reacts to the present crisis will tell us whether it has chosen to stand by the old Ireland or the new.

Eight years of legislative failure

"In the context of the eight years that have passed since the amendment was adopted... the failure by the legislature to enact the appropriate legislation is no longer unfortunate; it is inexcusable.

"What are pregnant women to do? What are the parents of a pregnant girl under age to do? What are the medical profession to do? They have no guidelines, save what may be gleaned from the judgements in this case.

"What additional considerations are there? Is the victim of rape, statutory or otherwise, or the victim of incest, finding herself pregnant, to be assessed in a manner different from others? The amendment, born of public disquiet, historically divisive of our people, guaranteeing in its laws to respect and by its laws to defend the right to life of the unborn, remains bare of legislative direction."

THIS IS NOT the statement, and these are not the questions, of a rampant liberal prodding his audience into a state of hysteria. It is Mr Justice Niall McCarthy in the Supreme Court giving his view of the failure of the Oireachtas to meet its responsibilities after the Eighth Amendment had become a provision of the Constitution in 1983.

It is tempting to say that the Supreme Court's reasoning has once more turned the world of legally enforced sexual morality on its head. But that would be to suggest that the consequences of the majority judgements delivered on Thursday are clear and undeniable; and they are not.

They have, instead, left the zealous opponents of abortion with a beached whale, gasping in the shallows of its own flawed logic. The very words on which they insisted, against the advice of the most senior law officer in the State, having been interpreted as providing for abortion in the Republic.

As Justice McCarthy said:

> "The terms of the Eighth Amendment now contained in Article 40.3.3° contemplate lawful abortion within the State. Despite the absence of regulating legislation, the judicial arm of Government must seek to enforce the guarantee. On the facts of this case, the mother is not to be prevented from having an abortion..."

This is precisely what the Des Hanafins, the William Binchys and the Bernadette Donners, the nodding bishops and winking politicians of the 1983 campaign, did not want to happen.

But the politicians who, like the bishops, had pretended to be otherwise engaged while their foot soldiers got on with the job of selling the amendment, failed to produce and pass the laws which would give their crude and clumsy wording a more precise meaning. Whether they did so because they believed the amendment would never be challenged, or through sheer embarrassment, it is difficult to say.

The Eighth Amendment, after all, was, in a sense, a vote of no confidence in the politicians themselves. It was written to prevent a Government, vulnerable to minority parties or its own wayward liberalism, from modifying or abandoning the legal prohibitions on abortion which had been in force for more than 120 years.

The amendment's authors were also worried by the risk that a Supreme Court of liberals appointed by such a government might prove receptive to arguments similar to those which eventually led to the removal of the legal ban on contraception here and the Supreme Court's decision on abortion in the United States in the 1970s.

The amendment, or so its proponents thought, would shut the door against all such political and judicial possibilities – or conspiracies as the organisers of SPUC and their clerical and political allies are apt to see any challenge to their view of the manner in which life is to be regulated.

The politicians who supported the wording in the Dáil were not only passing a vote of no confidence in themselves but in their successors and in a judiciary appointed by the President on the nomination of a government answerable to a parliament elected by the people.

They were not only shutting the door on conspiracies or on any deviation from the narrowest interpretation of an absolutist doctrine; they were blotting out any pretence at pluralism, any notion of republicanism and any acknowledgement of the legitimacy of any view but their own.

As Albert Reynolds sets his hand to reforming Fianna Fáil and establishing the character of his Government, he faces several challenges – chiefly those on unemployment and Northern affairs – which would test the courage, strength and ingenuity of an administration with a full Dáil term before it.

But his most immediate task, as the week's events proved, is to restore the confidence in politics which his predecessor did so much to undermine. Specifically, he must assert his own and his colleagues' determination to stand at arm's length from business or religious groups, each in its own way bent on usurping the functions of government.

He was roundly criticised last night for getting off to a bad start with the announcement of a Dáil committee instead of an unemployment forum; and he must know that the last thing the State now needs is more fudging and fumbling where openness and real involvement were promised.

He should be encouraged by the opinion polls showing a welcome for his Cabinet changes and signs of recovery in the party's fortunes. He cannot be under any illusion about the nature and intensity of the clerical and fundamentalist pressure aimed at throwing him off course as he begins to meet his first and potentially most serious challenge.

Even before the present case came to light, Dr Desmond Connell had written a pastoral letter in which he made an astounding comparison (hurriedly but not convincingly denied) between permissive legislation on abortion and abuses of power under the Nazis. It was as though he had forgotten the Holocaust or never knew how the Catholic Church had officially co-operated with several fascist regimes.

And after the judgements were delivered by the Supreme Court, Mrs Bonner announced – as though it were a virtue – that she trusted neither the court nor the legislators.

Mrs Bonner, Mr Hanafin and their allies favour a referendum rather than a legislative response to the State's present dilemma, trusting no doubt – as the hierarchy has always done – to the quiescence of politicians to see them through.

Maybe they should not be blamed. In addition to the 1983 referendum, they have two remarkable examples of cowardice and ineptitude to go on. The Norris judgement ordering the decriminalisation of certain homosexual acts was handed down in 1988; but neither the minority Fianna Fáil Government nor the Coalition has so far set about implementing it.

In 1973, the Supreme Court in the McGee case struck down, as unconstitutional, the law forbidding the importation, sale or advertising of contraceptives. A year later, Liam Cosgrave as Taoiseach led a small body of Fine Gael TDs across the Dáil to vote with Fianna Fáil against the Bill intended to fill the vacuum left by the Supreme Court's decision.

The Bill fell, the vacuum remained; and, in 1978, Mr Haughey came up with his laughable Irish solution to an Irish problem. Almost 20 years after the original decision, the Government is still dithering, wondering whether perhaps responsibility for the sale of condoms might be passed on to the health boards.

The only reason for any optimism about official action in the present case is that it now appears inextricably bound up with the referendum on the Maastricht Treaty.

JULY 11th, 1992

A novel victory for freedom of information

THE POLITICAL SYSTEM tottered to the verge of crisis (and back) yesterday as the Government attempted in the courts to block the work of the beef industry tribunal and, in the Dáil, opposition leaders wrestled with a constitutional puzzle which, to judge by his comments from Helsinki, is beyond the comprehension of the Taoiseach.

The trouble is this. Both the Government and the tribunal are creations of the Dáil. Both are accountable to it. The tribunal was established to inquire into matters which were not explained by the

Government to the Dáil's satisfaction. Some of these matters are (or are said to be) Cabinet decisions.

The Government – or its Fianna Fáil component – objects to the tribunal's inquiring into the manner in which these decisions were taken. That, it claims, would involve a breach of confidentiality. As Albert Reynolds said, it would make the Government's work impossible.

But, to block the questioning of current or former ministers, as the High Court was asked, would be to render the tribunal's mission impossible. Justice Liam Hamilton, its chairman, has made it clear that he needs to know about Cabinet decisions; indeed, it's obvious from the evidence to date that the information is crucial.

So, what the High Court was asked to decide yesterday was a dispute between two institutions, both answerable to the Dáil, both obliged to act in the public interest.

What the institutions think of each other was already more or less clear. Justice Hamilton had observed that, if certain questions had been answered in the Dáil, the tribunal would be unnecessary. Occasionally, in a wry aside, as when he said that ministers made decisions by looking into their own hearts, he appeared to be poking gentle fun at the politicians.

The Fianna Fáil view of the tribunal – because that, and not a Government view, is what we are talking about – was a good deal less complimentary. Séamus Brennan wondered at the sanctimoniousness and spoke of the hot air being generated and Mr Reynolds talked about "hearsay evidence" – although this is a statutorily established inquiry and the evidence is sworn.

But a more telling indication of the party's attitude to the inquiry is provided by its constant harping on the cost. Not only do its friends in some of the Sunday papers carry on sensationally about expense, but members of the Dáil – as in yesterday's interviews, Mr Reynolds himself – refer to the amounts being spent, especially on lawyers, in tones of populist regret.

It is as though Fianna Fáil was not a party to the tribunal's establishment and its erstwhile leader, Charles Haughey, had never promised that it would have the unreserved co-operation of the Government and all of the departments of State.

In fact, a Fine Gael deputy, Theresa Ahearn, has been informed by the Ceann Comhairle, Sean Treacy, that the cost to date amounts to £2.6 million, a far cry from the £40 million to which some of the commentators and deputies refer. The tribunal has been sitting for 110 days. Here are some comparable costs: Whiddy Island inquiry (71 days) £1 million; Stardust (123 days) £1.25 million; Kerry babies (82 days) £1.65 million, with £1.02 million in additional expenses.

And to get that same issue into still clearer perspective; first, the amounts of public money at stake in the relevant schemes ran into hundreds of millions of pounds; secondly, reliable sources say that the Revenue Commissioners have recovered, or are in the process of recovering, outstanding tax liabilities.

In other words, talk of the cost is – as the opposition leaders said in the Dáil yesterday – part of an attempt to denigrate the tribunal if its work cannot otherwise be frustrated.

Intrigued by the style and methods of decision making so far revealed in the tribunal, I turned the other day to an authority on this and related subjects: the book *Irish Government Today* by Sean Dooney, recently retired assistant secretary in the Department of Agriculture, and John O'Toole, a civil servant in the Department of Health.

One of the most intriguing features of their work was a short section on the workings of the Cabinet mysteriously headed 'Incorporeal Meetings'. This, I thought, had a theological flavour, attributable perhaps to the number of people with strong religious leanings who find their way into the higher echelons of the civil service. Here is what it had to say:

"Apart from the formal meetings, there are on occasion what are termed Incorporeal Meetings. These meetings relate to the conduct of unforeseen business which is so urgent as to require a decision before the next ordinary Government meeting. It is business of a type that does not require substantive discussion and is extremely unlikely to provoke disagreement...

"The procedure in such cases is that the Minister concerned prepares a brief note on the matter at issue which is circulated by the Government secretariat to all ministers available, together with a notification that an incorporeal meeting will be held to discuss the matter at a specific time.

"In practice, what then happens is that the secretary to the Government telephones all the ministers available at that time to get their agreement to what is proposed. The meeting is formally recorded as having taken place under the chairmanship of the Taoiseach, Tánaiste or most senior Government member available."

Here, several questions arise. The most obvious, which Justice Hamilton will now be in a position to have answered, is whether incorporeal meetings – or some refinement of them – were a common feature of the minority Fianna Fáil Government.

Some would go so far as to say that, if refinements were possible, they were the politicians to introduce them. Removing some of the more tangible elements of incorporeality seems an appropriate business for Mr Haughey and friends.

Given their performances to date and yesterday's dash to the High Court, I doubt if the politicians involved will readily and happily provide such information. Neither their training nor the system tends to openness. For all his huffing and puffing, Mr Reynolds is not going to change it, although he might look with profit beyond these shores.

The other day, an American academic called Jonathan Wiener was explaining to Pat Kenny how he'd come to find out so much about the FBI's spying on John Lennon. It was, he said, thanks to the Freedom of Information Act. "Not only does the Government belong to the people," said the professor, "Government information also belongs to the people."

The idea of official information belonging to the people is not only attractive but, in these parts, so novel as to verge on the revolutionary.

In Ireland, as we learn from the tribunal and some of the official or semi-official commentaries floating from the windows of Merrion Street, not only does the information not belong to the people, it seems increasingly obvious that it doesn't – and certainly didn't between 1987 and 1989 – belong to all the members of the Government.

But should not we, the taxpayers, be entitled to information about how our money was being spent or risked, gambled or invested in the late 1980s when Mr Goodman's business and that of the Government seemed inseparable; as Séamus Brennan and Ray Burke put it this week, when the national interest and that of the organisation coincided? Well, it seems not; or at any rate those who represent the State's interest – that's ours, isn't it? – at the tribunal don't think so. I was pleased that Justice Rory O'Hanlon thought otherwise.

DECEMBER 5th, 1992

Politicians living in terror of real change

IT'S MORE THAN a month since I heard Dr Gabriel Daly patiently explaining to Marian Finucane's devoted radio congregation that limbo no longer exists. What they'd learned all those years ago had become, as it were, theologically inoperative.

I wonder if he could now spare a couple of hours for some of the politicians and commentators who've been all of a dither since the election, as though at the latest news from whatever ecclesiastical council finally decided it was safe to stop torturing people who thought the world was round.

Their limbo, no less than that of Marian's more persistent callers, has become a casualty of the march of time. It's no longer the place where safely returned deputies spend their days, cracking jokes with old segocias before shuffling once more into the back benches for the start of the new Dáil.

Now it's a state of terror induced by uncertainty which, in turn, arises from the Dáil performing one of its essential functions: to elect a government. Except that on this occasion, as in 1989, the form is far from cut and dried; and the sound that keeps deputies awake at night is the plaintive echo of Charlie Bird, wondering why whatever's going to happen hasn't happened by newstime.

The dogs in the street are barking: the people voted for change. Even John Bruton, Des O'Malley and Michael Woods, all at several safe removes from the dogs in the street, say so. Commentators recycle their clichés to pass the message on and on but, as their importunate questions show, most of them haven't the faintest idea what it means.

However, when Dick Spring responds to this popular mood by aiming for real instead of cosmetic change and starts his round of discussions with Labour's near-neighbours in Democratic Left, the sound of indrawn breath is like a rush of wind through a tunnel.

Mr Bruton complains that Mr Spring is being unfaithful to the promise of a Rainbow Coalition which was set before the electorate during the campaign. Mr Bruton forgets:

(1) that it was he and not Mr Spring who made the promise;
(2) that Mr Spring repeatedly announced that no one was entitled to promise anything on his or Labour's behalf;

(3) that Mr Spring repeatedly insisted that what Labour stood for was full-blooded change; and

(4) that Mr Spring advised Labour voters to give their second or later preferences to Democratic Left and others of the left.

Forgetful Mr Bruton nodded and packed Jim Mitchell off to bat for Fine Gael. Mr Mitchell, looking puzzled, trotted out some of Fianna Fáil's old arguments against coalition and threw in one or two of his own. Like the one about Fine Gael, Labour and Democratic Left being able to muster no more than 83 votes.

But that was what Fianna Fáil and the Progressive Democrats had survived for three years and four months. Mr Mitchell said they were lucky; one of them might have died. And he looked more puzzled than ever. Fine Gael, he said, wasn't going to talk to Democratic Left anyway because the parties were poles apart ideologically.

He did not say how Fine Gael came to find itself in a position where it would take two partners, not one – unless of course the one was Fianna Fáil – to form a government with it. Fine Gael, it seemed, had lost 10 of its 55 seats *and* its memory, but not its natural superiority.

There was no question, never had been, about who should be Taoiseach in a government led by this very superior party. John Bruton, who was almost as unpopular as Albert Reynolds during the campaign, was the obvious man for the job. Dick Spring's proposal that the post of Taoiseach might rotate simply wouldn't work.

Another black hole in the public memory: it was not Mr Spring but Alan Dukes, then leader of Fine Gael, who'd first suggested the institution of a rotating Taoiseach. The suggestion, you may remember, was made to Fianna Fáil after the 1989 election; what you may not remember was that it was made at about the time that Fine Gael canvassed Democratic Left for support.

The Progressive Democrats, too, have been scathing about potential partners, and not only in the current round of negotiations, during which they've spent most of their time shouting advice or abuse from the sidelines. After the 1989 election, their most pungent comments were about Fianna Fáil, the party they said was unfit to govern.

The Progressive Democrats' 1989 comment was made a matter of days before the start of negotiations that ended in a historic coalition. It was an occasion for breaking moulds. Not any more, said Mr O'Malley. Not, at any rate, with Democratic Left.

At times like these, familiar figures occasionally show up in a new light. Mr O'Malley talks about banning opinion polls while campaigns are in progress, in the interests of small parties, of course. But small parties that are short of money usually avail of polls taken for publication: if they were banned, the bigger and better-heeled parties alone would have access to the information the polls provide. Democracy would not be served.

Then there was Pádraig Flynn on his way to a Cabinet meeting, craning from his official car to complain that the opposition was taking a long time about forming a rainbow coalition. He hisses and clicks, like a teacher of old mentioning something unpleasant; not at all like a Minister who's taken all summer and half the autumn to produce the wording that sank the abortion referendum.

But what is most striking is how politicians and commentators react to change or the possibility of change. During the election, the *Irish Independent* announced, on the most tenuous survey evidence, that Fianna Fáil had stopped the rot. It hadn't, of course. And neither has the paper.

On Thursday, an *Independent* editorial began:

"What game is Dick Spring playing at? He received a massive mandate from his new supporters to go into coalition. But the first thing he did was to start talking with the Democratic Left, a party with no policies which are widely attractive to the Irish electorate and one which has no track record of a constructive approach to government. Just why should Mr Spring pick that party to talk with first? He has the public baffled and not a little angry."

My recollection of the campaign is that Mr Spring's attitude to coalition was, as summarised here, that anyone who chose to include Labour in his plans was being presumptuous. Some people may well be baffled by the course of inter-party negotiations in the aftermath of an indecisive election. So are some of the politicians. But then neither politicians nor public are accustomed to change – especially of the kind that a doubling of Labour support suggests.

The information so far available from the Labour–Democratic Left discussions is not redolent with hints of revolutionary change; it suggests, rather, a serious attempt to undo some of the damage that has been inflicted on politics and some of the hardship that has been imposed on the vulnerable by largely conservative administrations.

Anyone who smugly believes that this isn't the case should look again at the other news of the week: three deaths, two from hypothermia, among Dublin's homeless; an estimated 900 housing repossessions sought this year; an extra 2,400 on the dole queues.

If, in tandem with Democratic Left or travelling alone, the newly strengthened Labour Party can persuade parties of the right or centre that it's time to stop regretting and start to change such conditions, it will have succeeded in bringing some light and hope to a State that has been short of both in the past five years.

It won't be easy, it won't be instant and it won't be done by people looking over their shoulders at their greedy sponsors.

Nothing is real in the real world

NO DOUBT YOU'VE taken to heart what Mr David Went had to say this week to the Institute of Bankers, of which he'd just become President. His inaugural address was reported in *The Irish Times* on Wednesday by my colleague, Mary Canniffe, under the fascinating headline: "Banks not charities, institute chief warns".

Banks, said Mr Went, are not the financial equivalent of the St Vincent de Paul or the Salvation Army; they are businesses which need profits to remunerate shareholders and to meet the needs of the country... Instead of knocking their profitability, people should be encouraged to say: "Well done, we need it."

As for the suggestion, from Peter Cassells and Bertie Ahern, that certain people (names supplied) had been involved in speculation, Mr Went said that bankers now knew how American actors felt in the 1950s: "Our industry, the business community in general and the Central Bank deserve better than McCarthyism. We are not speculators."

This boggled the mind. First, the news that the St Vincent de Paul Society was not, after all, charging 19.5 per cent on overdrafts; then, the banks had dropped their charitable work, doing good be stealth, as the character in *The Quare Fella* called it; now, it seemed the poor devils felt hounded – harried by the likes of Joe (or was it Colm?) McCarthy as if they were or had been up to their necks in subversion.

Mr Went acknowledged some failings. Banks had not promoted an understanding of some aspects of their affairs. They had been slow to provide proper transparency about services and prices. Opening hours of the associated banks had been poor. Big business borrowers had paid too little for their funds; they would find the new system more expensive.

As for the allegations of speculation, if bankers had not behaved legally or legitimately of late, so be it – let them be named, said Mr Went. But "the hysteria about anonymous people or institutions is… most unfair to those not concerned and indeed is a slur on the entire Irish business community as well as on the Central Bank, who have had no easy task in managing the markets over the last few months".

This is a complaint common to people in business, banking and politics. And, as Mr Went argues, it would be wrong of outsiders to assume that because some practitioners are suspect, everyone ought to be tarred with the same brush. But on the rare occasions when it's seriously suggested that any or all of these areas should be subject to closer scrutiny or made more amenable to public control, the hysteria comes, not from the critics, but from the defenders.

Mr Went's facetious reference to the St Vincent de Paul and the Salvation Army is a case in point. The risk of mistaking the Bank of Ireland for either organisation is really very slight. What he is responding to is the criticism that banks don't pay enough attention to the interests of the communities they exist in; and in this community of late some such criticism is widely thought to have been justified.

Business people and bankers respond to proposals of closer scrutiny or regulation by claiming that those who make the proposals don't know what they are talking about, that they are not living in the real world. The answer to the first line of defence is that it's hard to find well-informed critics when everything that can be done is done to keep the critics from informing themselves.

The real world argument is used, not to justify efficiency, or expertise, but to frighten off intruders. Real men don't eat quiche and those who know the real world also know that any attempt to modernise it will be met by flocks of squawking defenders who assure all and sundry that we're fine as we are. In any event, any attempt at change is bound to fail.

The real world, for instance, doesn't need reports about

improving the quality of women's lives, or the conditions in which they work, not because change is unnecessary but because it's likely to disturb the equilibrium. All manner of excuses will be offered – men will even go to the extreme of wheeling out Moore McDowell – to ensure that as many boreens as possible are visited on the way to a point at which no decisions are taken or no one knows what it was they set out to decide.

The real world doesn't want to hear about unemployment, because – as in the case of the report on women – to take it seriously would be to threaten the balance of power. Once raised to a level beyond that of mere debate, the problem would demand all sorts of action which would seriously damage the status quo. If you doubt this, just re-read the debates of the week on Mullaghmore, parliamentary reform and the introduction of a code of ethics for politicians.

Everyone agrees, for instance, about the need for parliamentary reform: a more efficient committee system, a more respectable workload for the Dáil; a degree of accountability which has been missing up to now. The committees are proposed by the most radically reforming Government in the history of the State.

The Government must be given credit for introducing the system, though it will take some time before it is fully functioning. But can it be that ministers will not, after all, be answerable to the committees as they are to the full Dáil? And the chairmanships of the four legislative committees are to be in the grasp of the governing parties: the opposition chooses to see this as a means of keeping some of the coalition's backbenchers busy and – more worrying – as a way to retain a degree of control that is inconsistent with the spirit of reform.

And why is it intent on limiting the role of the foreign-affairs committee to exclude (as I understand it) the State's negotiating positions, EC affairs and Northern Ireland? The limits on discussion of foreign affairs in the early decades of this State were imposed because of the suspicions that remained in the aftermath of the Civil War. Is it really necessary to leave us with this reminder of the bad old days, now that the thaw has come?

Then, of course, there is the question loosely described as ethics: declarations of interest, openness about sources of income, party funding, spending on elections and so on. These matters are properly under the control of parliaments in many, if not most, industrialised states. In theory, everyone here favours openness and accountability too.

Alan Dukes talks about peeping tommery and prying into the private affairs of politicians. By all accounts, many Fianna Fáil, Fine Gael and Progressive Democrat backbenchers say the system isn't necessary.

But what Mr Dukes calls prying in the case of TDs is regarded by many politicians as perfectly legitimate means testing when it happens to people on welfare.

As for the argument about codes of ethics being unnecessary, have we forgotten about the procession of scandals, the expensive inquiries, the disgrace to politics, the low opinions of the electorate...? Ah, sure, in the real world no one bothers about this kinda ting.

APRIL 10th, 1993

Late Late tries to turn the clock back

GERARD STEMBRIDGE'S *LOVECHILD* was given a vivid production at the Project Theatre in Dublin last year. Watching it during the election campaign, I thought it said more about the country than most of the speeches that were being churned out by the script factories.

Indeed, it was so much to the point, it should have toured every town in the country; if not with, then instead of, the politicians. This idea wasn't well received in the local snug, where idle chatter filled the time before the start of another unmemorable debate.

Could I imagine how the thing would go down in Ennis or Listowel? I was asked. (People who ask these questions always mutter "in the provinces" under their breaths, but take care not to tempt fate by antagonising touchy culchies.) The answer was yes, I could. It would go down every bit as well in Ennis or Listowel as it did in Dublin.

Lovechild is about a couple of teenage outsiders thrown together by Irish society and the way it might look at them and their unbidden predicaments.

She's been made pregnant by a friend of the family, but is so naive that when she's stopped on the way to England for an abortion she refuses to say she's really off to visit her granny. Insisting on the truth makes life awkward all round: she is taken off the boat and sent home.

His mother, who goes out to work to keep body and soul together, is not married either. She turns out to have been, of all things – you are not going to believe this – a bishop's mistress. But, of course, she hasn't seen his lordship since their affair ended, and when she tells her son the truth about his father he can't help fretting: wondering what the bishop feels about him and why they had never met.

The youngsters are plagued by conventional friends and damned by a shrill chorus, dressed in pink plastic macs and high pointed pixies, whose job is to see that nothing happens and, if anything does, to make sure that everyone feels good and guilty about it.

When the lad finally gets to visit his father, what he meets is a ventriloquist's dummy operated by a trendy priest with an impenetrable line in clerical cliché. He doesn't get around to singing 'Do You Want Your Ould Lobby Washed Down?' but it's touch and go. The trendy one's other noticeable characteristic is that he reverses the normal practice – kisses the ground and walks on women.

It's all very far-fetched, of course. Even a member of the cast complains about how outlandish it is. Why can't writers be more down to earth – more true to life? More in tune with the Ireland we know in the 1990s? The very questions they ask in the snug before the conversation drifts over more speculative ground.

Whatever happened to that chap, Stembridge? Used to write scripts for *Scrap Saturday* about politicians with delusions of grandeur and the endearing toadies who followed them around. Fellows who had it hard – oh, lashed by the Brothers – and women beavering away on an inside track of the National Sleaze.

The crowd in RTÉ were on to him, of course. They had his number. (That name, by the way, Stembridge. Is it Irish at all?) Of course, the stuff he was doing was funny enough in its own way, but it just wasn't *us*.

I mean, if tourists happened to tune in, it'd be bound to give them the wrong impression: make us out to be a very shifty lot altogether, and still stuck in the rut we were in 40 years ago. But you can't whack the boys in Montrose, always on the lookout with the old national interest in mind. I mean, Fianna Fáil, the Catholic Church and the GAA have their rights, too.

Yes, we have changed, and not only in the last 40 years. The change has been mostly for the better and has been achieved largely by citizens, young and old and in all quarters, making up their own minds about the direction to be taken. Indeed, one of the encouraging things about the past week has been the way in which many – perhaps most? – people reacted to what seemed an attempt on the *Late Late Show* to turn the clock back.

I wrote here last week about a worry shared by many in the last couple of years – a feeling that they had been let down by some of the leading representatives of God, Mammon and politics in whom they had been taught to place their trust. Now, it looks as if people who placed trust of a certain kind in the *Late Late Show* have been let down as well.

Whether they took 'her side' or not, they had expected a straightforward interview with Annie Murphy, conducted by someone they had come to regard as at best an agent of change and at least as a smoothly professional operator whose concern for the programme's reputation, if nothing else, ensured that – even in search of controversy – he remained more or less on the middle ground.

Instead, what they got – and appear not to have forgiven during the week – was a performance which drew on the moods, humours and prejudices of the 1950s and early 1960s and flew in the faces of those who nowadays respond to commentaries on the still unequal place of women in Irish society as the exaggerations of cranks.

Not only the tone, but the content was from the past. A past in which women were always out for the one thing (wink and nod) and, worse, when they got it – after reducing the man to their level – ran off and complained. It was what made them either unfit to rear a child or fit for little else.

For his part, you could always be sure that, even when he signed on the dotted line and admitted paternity, the man was not the author of – and often a reluctant partner in – his own misfortune. As a rule, especially if he was a strong farmer's son and she a labourer's daughter, it was certain he'd been caught, trapped, ensnared. And if he were a bishop...

I haven't read Annie Murphy's book, but found Nuala O'Faolain's account of her life in *The Irish Times* a sad and moving story. It spoke, you may recall, not of Jezebel but of a child growing up under the familiar shadows of a drunken, self-righteous father and a pitiful, boozy mother.

When her own marriage failed, and she was sent to Ireland to stay with Éamon Casey, Annie Murphy seems to have been not so much a temptress on the prowl as a woman hurt and in need of care. No doubt she makes the most of her story. But, on television and in such interviews as I've read, she appears far from scheming. Instead, she looks slightly puzzled, but ready to accept the attacks made on her.

On the *Late Late Show*, the attacks came not only from some members of the audience, but from a presenter who claimed he "just knew" Dr Casey's mind on some issues at least. But, as the nagging, niggling argy-bargy about moons and cars and hair-washing went on, no one bothered to point out that the bishop had acknowledged his son and hadn't stayed around long enough to give his version of the story.

I was in Waterford when the programme, which was repeated on Channel 4 on Monday evening, was first broadcast. And it was astonishing to emerge from a Labour conference, where so many hopes were pinned on the party's ability to influence the modernisation of Irish society, to be met by waves of anger from people who believed that what they'd just seen on television represented a step or two backwards.

People in bars, restaurants and hotels were virtually unanimous – not only about how the programme had been handled, but why they thought it wrong. A man from Waterford Glass, out for a quiet beer with his wife, expressed the views of many when, without prompting of any sort, he vowed to telephone RTÉ on Monday to let Mr Byrne know how angry he felt.

It was then I began to recall Gerard Stembridge's *Lovechild* and to wish again that people all over the country could enjoy its salty humour and its celebration of love.

Flying the flags for dangerous certainties

IT MAY BE that people who need people are, as the song goes, the luckiest people in the world. Leaders who need enemies are something else – opposition is the name of their game – without something or someone to oppose, they must rummage for a reason to exist.

Nationalist movements are often based solely on opposition during their struggles for independence. Too often they are left high and dry when the struggle succeeds.

This is almost invariably the case when taking charge of its country's affairs is the height of the movement's ambition, and the answer to the question "what next?" is uncomplicated by plans for social or economic reform: "Now we run the show for a change."

The same sense of not knowing where to turn may take hold of the leaders of older states, colonisers as well as colonised. It usually happens when they drum up support on the strength of exaggerated or imagined threats from abroad – only to find that they've suddenly vanished and with them the basis for some grand defensive strategy.

But what is most objectionable, and potentially most dangerous, in nationalism is the feeling of certainty it can instil in people: the certainty that excludes others simply because they haven't been born here, don't speak the language, are not part of the history, don't subscribe to the rules of the political, religious or cultural club outside which there is no salvation.

The price of membership to this exclusive club is nothing less than conversion – a form of cultural immersion during which the subject is washed clean of any trace of previously held opinions or old identity.

At best, nationalism is an expression of stubborn independence based on the common interests of the national community. It is sufficiently confident of its place in the world to accept inter-dependence.

At worst, it not only imagines threats from across the borders; it is so convinced of their reality that it feels impelled to move in, flags flying, to eliminate them.

In this country, we are so used to politicians playing the nationalist card that neither we nor they think twice about it. "When in doubt start a row with the British" is a piece of advice not quite as old as "England's difficulty is Ireland's opportunity", but twice as foolish.

We are, however, much better at spotting others' follies than we are at admitting our own; and we are not alone in this: there is a nationalist card in every hand, and a religious card in most, if politicians or commentators choose to use them.

During the crisis provoked by Iran's capture of American hostages in the 1980s, people in the Washington hotel we stayed in rushed downstairs after watching the evening news and growled about sending out their boys "to nuke the bastards". When we asked them where they thought Iran was, they didn't know.

These hotel guests – whose sentiments were shared by several of the State Department officials with whom we had dinner – couldn't be sure whether their warheads should be aimed north, south, east or west of the Potomac. But they sure as hell knew what to do with poor Jimmy Carter when he failed to live up to expectations nourished by commentators and the opposition.

Mr Carter had enemies, at home and abroad. His trouble was that he botched his sole attempt to deal with the foreigners to the satisfaction of the folk who had never crossed their state line. I suppose it could be said that enemies were wasted on him. George Bush was determined not to make the same mistake in Kuwait, but he flunked the final test.

Britain, too, has had her moments of nationalist ecstasy – and her dolled-up enemies. Few of these were better wrapped for instant exploitation than the comic opera general Leopoldo Galtieri of Argentina. He was only trying to distract attention from domestic problems when he sent his men to masquerade as scrap merchants in South Georgia before crossing to the Falklands.

But, given our own predilections, and the curious attitude of the Government of the day, the memory that lives with people here is of Margaret Thatcher hoarsely egging her troops on towards Goose Green, Port Stanley and – though this was still on the horizon – a tub-thumping, flag-waving Tory victory in a general election she might otherwise have been hard-pressed to win.

Now, as commentators analyse the collapse of one EC project (the exchange rate mechanism of the European Monetary System) and anticipate a substantial threat to another (economic and monetary union), we are faced again with the consequences of nationalism; all the more worrying because it is the nationalism of great powers, not of those who have little more than nuisance value.

France and Germany, whose leaders were the authors of the EMS and the ERM, became close allies, twin pillars of the European Community, not only because they shared a desire to avoid another world war but because they wanted to be on the winning side if the Cold War, either by accident or design, turned to shooting.

Their united front was at least partly inspired by an external threat, real enough to begin with, and played for all it was worth for several years. But in the end kept going by those on either side of the Berlin Wall who thought an external threat more effective than any amount of rhetorical guff about the primacy of the state or the supremacy of market forces.

The full effects of Germany's unification and reorientation remain to be measured, both in the EC and in the wider world. Some senior commentators take the view that France, rather than the community's peripheral states, has been the first casualty of the change. They expect the new leadership in Paris to become, for the time being at least, more nationalistic and more intransigent.

The collapse of Stalinism in central and eastern Europe left people on both sides of the wall flat-footed, even if it is only now becoming apparent how accurate were the warnings of some politicians and commentators who said the results would prove as big a challenge to the West as to those left to pick up the pieces in Moscow, Tblisi or Kiev.

The West, which often encouraged the nationalists of eastern Europe during the Cold War, was clearly unprepared for the re-emergence of nationalism in its most virulent form once the disintegration of the Stalinist states began. Nationalism, fuelled by old enmities, some of which had lain in wait for 60 years, was exacerbated by religious feelings which had long been dormant or scarcely expressed.

It is astonishing that these happenings should have been greeted in this country with surprise; shameful that, as people who have experienced the consequences of civil strife for so long, we had not been more active in the European Community on behalf of those who are paying an appalling price for the same kind of vanity and folly elsewhere.

And it's disgraceful that our Government should tag along in the wake of others who can't decide what to do about former Yugoslavia; and try to assuage their guilt and satisfy their citizens by pathetic public-relations gestures towards the children of Bosnia.

Reduce expectations and place all cards face up on the table

FIFTY YEARS AGO, George Orwell wrote a stinging piece about the baleful influence of language on politics. And, although he was particularly concerned with such current issues as the impact of Stalinism on Western thinking, what he had to say is relevant still.

"If thought corrupts language," he wrote, "language can also corrupt thought." And his point is demonstrated again and again in the public affairs of the 1990s where language may be used, not to clarify, but to bend or obscure thought, often with carefully judged intent.

The effects of this range from a relatively harmless cloud of confusion spread by technical or bureaucratic jargon to a dangerous sense of exclusion – the suspicion that the fate of a group or class is decided by people who are indifferent to its interests and use the language to camouflage their intentions.

The harmless version is the kind of stuff labelled nonsensical by the cheerful woman from Liverpool, who runs the Plain English Campaign. She handed out a Gold Bull Award this week to a department which dreamed up the description "a device or arrangement that may be used to permit a patient to lie down" for a hospital bed.

I am not sure whether our own beloved bureaucrats use the same definition, but I heard Eamon Hannan of the Western Health Board, the other day, making a distinction between male beds and female beds. Proving, I suppose, that in this country almost anything can he reduced to sex.

But there is no doubt that in that great treasure house of Bull, the ranks of management, the Irish are well up to international standards.

Your average Irish manager is as willing as the next man (or woman) to slide down a learning curve and run his thoughts past you so that you can take them on board when you, in turn, hit the ground running and make for the bottom line.

No doubt, keeping pace with this frenetic activity, regular reports of managerial and marketing affairs are peppered with references to players where no self-respecting footballer has ever set foot, and level playing pitches are demanded by people whose habits would make the All Blacks seem genteel.

The left has changed a great deal since Orwell's day – with the rise of the Labour Party and the fall of Stalinism – but in its remoter areas it still clings to some of its old lingo, the kind that gets more impenetrable the deeper you plunge into the ideological thicket.

I once reported a by-election in Cavan–Monaghan where a candidate of the far left had decided to stand and, on a Saturday morning in Monaghan Town, turned up to hand out his manifesto to the shoppers. One old couple put down their heavy message bags, rummaged for their glasses and slowly read. From the top left-hand corner to the bottom right crawled the serpentine demons of the left: lackeys of imperialism, running dogs of capitalism, *comprador* classes slithering about in the shadows of the commanding heights of the economy.

When the old couple finished reading, they folded the paper and handed it back to its author, the representative of the Communist Party of Ireland (Marxist–Leninist). Then they thanked him for his trouble and moved off murmuring: "It's all right sir, sure we're Protestants ourselves."

Nowadays, politicians employ people to write their jargon for them. Take the senior British civil servant who gave evidence lately to the Scott Inquiry now investigating the sale of arms-making equipment to Iraq. When the question was first raised in the House of Commons, any such sale was denied by a succession of ministers who came up with a series of ingenious answers that appeared to address the issue; but skilfully managed to avoid telling the truth.

Asked about this at the inquiry, the civil servant who had devised many of these replies happily explained to his lordship that an answer to a parliamentary question was an art form, not necessarily a means of communication.

It was a clever description and much was made of it on Wednesday when Margaret Thatcher became the first British Prime Minister, past or present, to appear before such an inquiry. For it was clear that some of the parliamentary answers prepared for her had been, in another famous phrase, economical with the truth.

The art form, however, is neither confined to Westminster nor to the Thatcher years. Here, too, we have been afforded a glimpse of the back-room boys at work on their masters' behalf, courtesy of another tribunal and another judge: Mr Justice Liam Hamilton and his inquiry into the beef industry.

You may need to be reminded of the tale of a civil servant who, during Dáil exchanges in the early days of the affair, was given a pat on the back for throwing an inquisitive deputy off the scent with a clever, but diversionary, reply.

And although misleading the house never was the hanging offence in Dublin that it used to be in London, the public memory is hardly so short that we have already forgotten Dick Spring's pursuit of Charles Haughey on the subject of a certain meeting with Bernie Cahill.

The business on that occasion was Greencore. It took Mr Spring five attempts to get to the facts. You must remember Mr Haughey's famous reply – "Oh, *that* meeting" – if only because it might so easily have been given more recently by a different politician in another place.

Sir Patrick Mayhew and John Major were caught flat-footed on the question of contacts with the Provisional IRA and Sinn Féin. More would have been made of it, too, had not their defenders been able to appeal to what is sometimes described as the national interest.

We have now reached the point where the use or abuse of language advances from the mildly amusing or the procedurally questionable, to the simply misleading. And danger increases at every step of the way.

It is hardly surprising that many in Northern Ireland are in a state of nerve-wracking uncertainty. Quite apart from the paramilitaries of all shapes, who step from the wings to murder this one for his religion or that one for the uniform, some feel threatened and few are much encouraged by the news they read or hear.

Today's *Irish Times*/Coopers & Lybrand poll shows the unionists more uneasy than the nationalists. That, too, is unsurprising – they have been told lies in London and suspect that in Dublin there is a conspiracy against them. Some of their own leaders, John Taylor and Peter Robinson, issue warnings that sound like threats; and the assurances offered by the South seem ambiguous, to say the least.

The North's cleverest politician, John Hume, insists that the proposals he has agreed with Gerry Adams pose no threat to anyone. But Mr Adams, after almost 25 years of violence for which the IRA bears substantial responsibility, has begun to sound like an elder statesman. He has started to lecture others on the subject of peace.

It is as if peace was not a condition to be achieved by everyone working together; but a slogan invested with the values of the picket. Much as 'life' is adapted by the opponents of a woman's right to choose as the standard of the pro-life campaign. Is anyone who opposes the campaign automatically anti-life? Is anyone who questions Hume–Adams anti-peace?

Mr Hume, however, steadfastly refuses to publish his proposals; but insists that Britain holds the key to the solution he offers. Albert Reynolds, too, speaks of processes, time frames, windows of opportunity. Peace and politics, he seems to suggest, are not the same thing: you can have one without the other.

Mr Spring, meanwhile, says that an internal settlement in the

North is not enough and appears to contradict his own principles by asking the British Government to recognise not only the legitimacy but the value of aspiring to unity. Others put it more bluntly, expecting Britain to persuade the unionists that their best interests lie outside the union of which Britain itself is part.

It is time expectations were reduced, definitions more clearly spelled out and everyone's cards were placed face up on the table.

AUGUST 13th, 1994

The night when the shooting started

MY MOST VIVID memory of the night the shooting started in Belfast was of a thin-faced man with frightened eyes standing outside his house on the Crumlin Road. He seemed to be talking to himself as the crowd surged past, retreating from Hooker Street and the shock of fire from the B Specials' whippets.

"Not again," he whispered. "Jesus Christ, not again." And he stood in the half-light, old enough to have seen the fighting in the 1920s and the 1930s, more shaken than anyone else.

All that week, attention had been on Derry and on the need, as the word on the grapevine had it, to take the heat off the Bogside. There had been disturbances – inspired by the grapevine in nightly television reports – in several towns and villages from Toomebridge to Newry.

In Belfast, there were attacks on Hastings Street RUC Station and, more spectacularly, on the car showrooms of Isaac Agnew, which went up in flames. Who organised the attacks was not clear, but senior RUC officers later told Mr Justice Scarman how they believed they were facing a planned and widespread rising.

Certainly, as the week went by and the struggle in the Bogside became more intense, old enemies in Belfast began to view each other with renewed suspicion. Already there had been some fighting in the city: flimsy barricades had been thrown up at the Crumlin Road end of Hooker Street and many families had left their houses, either to go away on holidays, or to take refuge with relatives who lived in safer places.

The RUC officers may have believed that a rising was imminent; reporters from the national newspapers in Dublin had a very different impression. They shared with the Catholics of west and north Belfast a feeling of imminent doom, which somehow seemed closer with the arrival on the streets of the B Specials.

But nothing, not even the death of John Gallagher in Armagh, who was the first to have been shot, prepared us for the ferocity of the attacks which overwhelmed so many small streets in the Falls, Clonard and Ardoyne areas of Belfast on the night of August 14th, 1969.

I recall Hooker Street in particular because, as far as I know, it was one of the first to have been attacked. It was also close enough to Cliftonpark Avenue, where I'd lived for over six months 10 years earlier, to be at least relatively familiar.

Now nothing seemed familiar as we approached from the lower end of the Crumlin Road. The streetlights had been turned off or smashed. Crowds were growling in the darkness where Protestant Disraeli Street joined the main road. Almost opposite, Hooker Street was still barricaded but, for a moment, strangely quiet. There were shadowy figures in the background.

Our little company – two *Irish Times* colleagues, Jack Fagan and Jill Smyth, Kevin Healy of RTÉ and a cheerful Norwegian broadcaster called Willy – passed on tiptoe in what must have seemed a caricature of normality. Then we cowered by a wall as the Disraeli Street crowd, urged on by men wearing white armbands, swarmed across the road.

Whether the invaders from Disraeli Street were ambushed by the defenders of Hooker Street, I cannot remember. Next day, it seemed they had attacked both occupied and empty houses indiscriminately, although only a few bore signs of fire. On that balmy night, smoke and the sound of breaking glass were everywhere.

Now and then it was almost quiet. We could hear the crunch of boots on broken glass, the thud of bodies colliding, and someone shouted "bastards" again and again.

We were still at the corner of the street, sheltering by a barred window, when the sound of the crowd took on a more ominous note.

Armoured cars had suddenly appeared on the Crumlin Road, their machine guns swivelling in the turrets, menacing those who stood, ran or lay in the streets. The cars turned into Hooker Street and, in a nightmare of muffled noise – voices of engines and people mixed – the shooting began.

I can't say we followed the noise down Hooker Street to find out what was happening, because by now armoured cars seemed to be arriving from all directions. They were coming down, as well as up, the Crumlin Road and, although they may have been the same vehicles making a circuit, it was beginning to dawn on us that the guns and the shooting were real.

There were signs, too, that the fighting had spread across the city. Someone arrived and said there was shooting in several parts of the Falls Road. A terrified young man begged a lift in the car we were using. In the International Hotel where we stayed, close to the City Hall, several messages had been left with the receptionist and the night porter, telling us of dead and injured. (One young man had been killed in Hooker Street.)

We were taking it in turns to answer calls from politicians and community leaders and to check such information as we could with the RUC. One of the most chilling messages was from the chairman of the Northern Ireland Civil Rights Association (NICRA), Frank Gogarty. He phoned at about two in the morning with a list of events and casualties. And an appeal to Dublin for help.

Although we had spent hours writing and rewriting our own

reports, trying to separate fact from rumour, wondering what weight was to be attached to official accounts of events, it was still a shock to hear on the early-morning radio news that five people had been killed and more than 100 injured during the night.

Reports from Derry spoke of the arrival of British troops and the welcome given them by the people of the Bogside. They would soon be in Belfast – and made equally welcome in Catholic areas – although by then a whole street would have been set on fire and a great shift of population would have begun.

In the weariness and elation of the morning, we too were beginning to recognise – but only vaguely – the challenges that the night had raised, to unionism, nationalism and the civil-rights movement, to the British and Irish governments and, above all, to the people of this island.

AUGUST 20th, 1994

Is there no room in the slammer for TDs?

SEVERAL YEARS AGO, I telephoned a friend in Washington to ask where I might find a certain member of the United States Senate. The friend, a journalist who works for a news magazine, said I was out of luck. He knew where the senator was but not when he could be contacted.

"You see," he said, "he's in the slammer." And so he was, with almost half of his State legislature who'd been engaged in some political scam when the authorities caught up with them. My friend is American-Irish but still keeps an eye on the old sod; and it amused him that an Irish journalist should have been surprised at the senator's fate.

He was even more surprised that the authorities here had not already laid hands on some of our own, although in the international league of political hooks, crooks and bottlewashers, he tends to place the Irish among the bottlewashers. Maybe he suffers from an inferiority complex. Or Tammany Hall has slipped his mind.

I felt like giving him a call the other night when I heard that two members of Bill Clinton's treasury team, Roger Altman and Jean Hanson, had resigned – apparently for no better reason than that they'd misled congressional committees by giving them incomplete or conflicting accounts of their parts in the so-called Whitewater affair.

I knew he'd have been amused to hear about the Hamilton Report and the nest of ministers who, it would appear, misled the Dáil in the 1980s; some have now been joined by colleagues in a strenuous effort to mislead the public in the tribunal's aftermath. And without so much as a hint of apology, let alone resignation.

What aftermath? You may well ask. There is no aftermath. This is a country where the game of consequences is never played. Life is a continuation of those old-time schools where all that mattered was that you got away with it, whatever it was.

Hardly anyone resigns. Few are fired. Occasions on which politicians are brought to book are so few and far between that the only people likely to remember them are faithful followers of the pub quiz. Misleading the Dáil is not an offence, it's an achievement. Civil servants are praised for supplying ministers with puzzling answers.

The idea that anyone of note in public life (politics or business) should end up in the slammer is unthinkable. A government may break the law; senior people in a company may become involved in schemes of tax evasion; risks may be taken with public funds or the State's most important industry; and people may play ducks and drakes with the schemes and property of the European Union. The slammer is for serious criminals like shoplifters.

Our parliament retains the Victorian trappings of the English – the pomposity and quaint procedure, which often protects the guilty and frustrates the questioner – while avoiding any serious attempt at modernisation. To adapt a much-abused phrase, we've inherited everything English bar their sense of honour.

That system relies – or relied until some of Mrs Thatcher's boys got their hands on it – on the assumption that ministers told the truth. If, somehow, they misled parliament, they made a clean breast of it, apologised and, usually without delay, resigned. There were few exceptions to the rule. It was, as we have just seen, one of the practices which the Americans wisely adopted.

If the system were strictly applied here, there would have been a few vacancies in the Government of the late 1980s and some of the present ministers might well be challenged to repeat inside the Dáil the statements they've been making on radio and television. As it is, the serious penalties in the Republic are for breaking the rules of a parliamentary party, not for misleading the Dáil. Party before parliament, it seems, and it speaks volumes for our attitudes to parliamentary democracy.

But as Mr Justice Hamilton stressed, and it's necessary to go on repeating, if questions had been answered in the Dáil, there would have been no need for the tribunal; if ministers had been taking the business of parliamentary democracy seriously, we wouldn't be wasting time and money now.

And if it hadn't been for Pat Rabbitte, Dick Spring, Des O'Malley, Tomás Mac Giolla, Pat O'Malley and Barry Desmond, we would be in deeper trouble than we are now. Now, at least, the Oireachtas has been given an opportunity to reassert its primacy and the Labour Party has a chance to redeem its reputation and insist on reform.

If the Government is to convince the electorate that it's taking Hamilton to heart, it will have to come up with a specific programme and a realistic timetable for its implementation. It will have to take on issues on which Hamilton makes recommendations and issues where he leaves it up to the politicians to decide what is to be done.

In the second category there is, for instance, the central issue of the funding of political parties. The report considers the present practice of receiving huge contributions from companies in the beef industry "normal" and leaves it at that. Yes, it is common practice and to that extent normal, but is it good for democracy in this State in the 1990s?

Mr Spring has already suggested that he considers it a matter of great significance. So it is. Now is the time to do something about it.

Fianna Fáil won't like the introduction of the subject. Neither, I suspect, will many people on the opposition benches. It will have to be tackled. So far, this Government and this Dáil have had a lousy record of taking on tough issues: if they don't start now, they might as well give up the ghost.

It would be yet another irony if one of the few monumental marks left by the present affair were to be its extraordinary by-product, the decision restricting Cabinet confidentiality in a manner which the late Walter Ulbricht might have envied and Franz Kakfa might have exquisitely described.

There is, of course, a powerful lobby in favour of doing nothing at all or as little as possible to meet the challenge of Hamilton. They would make what changes may be required, say, in the Department of Agriculture, or by order of the European Union, and leave it at that.

I've heard people who say that they know what farmers are thinking and that they are content: Goodman pays well and pays on the nail, that's all that matters. And farmers, they say, are the people who count.

This is the kind of rubbish that once made the TB eradication scheme a byword for bottomless pits and drove a wedge between urban and rural communities on questions of tax. I suspect it's a view that many who live on or by the land do not share. It's too close for comfort to the feckless husbandman caricatured by H L Mencken – the only member of the community, he said, who was handed money from the public purse and when his venture failed came back for more, and was given more because he was still considered the salt of the earth.

Generosity drowns in triumphalism

WATCHING THE SHOW at Government Buildings on Tuesday, it was hard to tell whether this was a great political occasion or a rerun of the Offaly team on its way home after winning the All-Ireland final.

But there were some notable differences between the events. The Offaly players paid generous tribute to their rivals, Limerick. In Merrion Street, the reassuring message meant for unionists and commended by John Hume was drowned in a chorus of triumphalism.

The Offaly crowd was in no doubt about its cause for celebration. As far as can be judged, public reaction to the Merrion Street meeting has been less euphoric, more confused; hopeful certainly, but in places tinged with suspicion. The questions "Why now?" and "Will it last?" have been raised in many minds and for obvious reasons.

The announcement of the Provisional IRA ceasefire had all too conveniently diverted attention from what promised, in the debate on the Beef Tribunal Report, to be the most serious parliamentary examination of public affairs in this State since the Arms Crisis of the 1970s.

Suspicions provoked by the coincidence might have been dismissed if it had not been for the crowing of the Coalition's supporters when they heard that the debate on the tribunal report – for which Fianna Fáil had assembled an array of half-baked arguments – was about to be overshadowed.

Then, as if to prove that the Tuesday show was another rushed affair, it became clear the Government had not given the slightest thought to the Forum for Peace and Reconciliation – the route by which Gerry Adams and Sinn Féin were to enter constitutional politics. The Government's plan seems to have been written on a single sheet.

Then there was Albert Reynolds' acknowledgment that he had not yet written to the unionists about the forum, which begs a question about its title: reconciliation with whom?

More ominously, Gerry Adams' answers and evasions when he was persistently questioned by Brendan O'Brien on RTÉ's *Prime Time* cast doubt on the intentions of the republican movement and, even as Mr Adams complained tetchily about "quibbling", suggested that clarification of the status of the ceasefire is of more than academic interest.

It took Seamus Mallon, whose common sense has not deserted him, to wonder for a moment how the show in Merrion Street (the Adams interview had yet to come) must have looked to outsiders, especially those who had lost relatives and friends in the violence of the last 25 years.

But imagining the impact on others was the last thing on the minds of those who wrapped the green flag round them outside Government Buildings. The impression they created – least of all on the people Mr Mallon had in mind – was less important than the messages sent to Mr Adams' supporters in west Belfast or their cousins in the Bronx, who may also be in some doubt about the "complete cessation of military operations".

Constituents have to be reassured on all sides, including those of Mr Adams, who have to move from the walled simplicities of fundamentalism to a world in which they may be questioned and criticised without fear of reprisal – because that is or ought to be the essence of constitutional politics. And they may not be getting the best example from their neighbours and new allies in Fianna Fáil of late.

Failure to accept the otherness of others is a fault of both sides in this country. Unionists have displayed their version of it for decades – and cannot be allowed to hope that, if and when the dust settles, they will return to their old ways.

Southern nationalists, as might be expected, have their own

version which, as you may have gathered, was on display on Tuesday. Unionists, they say, have every right to their opinions and to a place on this island provided they do not really want to behave as unionists or to take their unionism seriously.

The theory is that unionists are really Irish but, due to some accident of birth or peculiarity developed in later life, they stubbornly insist on imagining themselves British. This in itself is no harm – if they don't try to act on it. The real demons are those who led or duped them into their present condition or who now contrive to keep them in captivity.

This notion of unionism was once well served by Brookeborough and the landed gentry. Its urban representative was in the hard-headed businessman whose word was undoubted and who, if he was civil and liked a jar, was as near as dammit one of our own, or at any rate on the point of turning. The working-class unionist, now as ever, is the enigma.

But just when you hope that people on either side of the border are about to change, you find yourself face to face with an example that proves you wrong.

Fianna Fáil, for instance, to judge by its performances in the past fortnight, seems determined to show that – for all its abandonment of core values – it has changed little in the last 30 years, maybe longer. During what passed for a debate on the Beef Tribunal Report, it gave as solid a display of stonewalling as the Dáil has seen since the days of Kevin Boland and Neil Blaney.

Then as if to feed the nostalgia of those who long for the bad old days, there was the case of Susan O'Keeffe. Once, when rampant moneylending was investigated by RTÉ's current affairs programme, *Seven Days*, a tribunal was set up – to investigate the programme, not the moneylending – and, while a researcher was made to carry the can, the lenders carried on as before.

The fact that Susan O'Keeffe, who helped shed light on a much bigger scandal, is now threatened with arrest and imprisonment, is a shameful reflection on politicians of all shades, but especially on those who pretended to be modernisers in backward-looking parties in a shifty trade where all that matters is staying in power and keeping the foot soldiers happy.

Cheerleaders from the beef tribunal debate, such as Charlie McCreevy, once masqueraded as backbench modernisers in Fianna Fáil. Whenever Mr McCreevy was in danger of being forgotten, he would announce that what Fianna Fáil needed was straight talk – on everything but the North.

Needless to say, Mr McCreevy was the man to shoot from the hip, tell it as it was or administer whatever cliché happened to be fashionable at the time. And he might have been doing it still if his circumstances had not taken a sudden change for the better.

Now, with the help of ministerial office, he has convinced himself that the last thing the party needs is straight talk – or, indeed, any talk at all about Mr Justice Hamilton's report – while, on the national question, he has found soulmates in Sinn Féin.

Mr McCreevy is not alone, merely following Mr Reynolds' lead. Ever since he became convinced that it was possible to secure an IRA ceasefire and Sinn Féin support for the Downing Street Declaration, the Taoiseach has adopted the vocabulary of the Provos and a fair approximation of their attitudes.

But some expressions like "demilitarisation" change meaning with every echo chamber they pass through. What seems neutral, if vaguely technical, in one area has a distinctly sinister ring to it in another. It depends on who's speaking and who's listening.

John Hume presumably knows what he means by "a new and agreed Ireland", but not everyone else does; and when he becomes paired with Mr Adams, politically speaking, those who had always feared his intelligence begin to suspect the worst.

For some time after Mr Reynolds' arrival in office, what he said and how he said it had the merit of novelty in Belfast and London. Politicians and commentators developed the habit of saying that, unlike his predecessor and some of his colleagues, he carried no historical baggage; and they thought he was all the better for that.

As his vocabulary changed, suspicion grew. Fianna Fáil, it seemed, was reverting to type: in no time at all, some fear, it will be back where it was in the 1920s: a semi-constitutional party once again. Which may make Mr Adams and his friends feel more at home, but is bound to add to the awkwardness of relations with Britain and make it difficult to convince the unionists of the Government's good faith.

It will also confuse or worry a lot of people in the South who thought we had all moved beyond the wilder shores of nationalism; people who may fear that, if Sinn Féin and its new allies manage to avoid calling the ceasefire permanent, sooner or later they may attempt to change another word which seems central to the achievement of peace – consent.

NOVEMBER 19th, 1994

Time for Fianna Fáil to look into its own heart

IT WAS AN extraordinary chain of events. At one end, in the shadows, sat the people who, in childhood, had been sexually abused by a Catholic priest, given access to them by trusting parents or teachers – familiar figures of authority in a society which wouldn't hear a word said against the Church, much less an accusation of paedophilia against one of its ministers.

At the other end of this extraordinary chain, a Government collapses; a Taoiseach, his ministers and a senior judge resign; political, legal and clerical establishments are under siege and the country totters through a crisis of authority, the likes of which has not been experienced for almost 25 years.

Between the two – the victims and their would-be defenders – there is a world of ambiguity and evasion where nothing is faced if it can possibly be avoided, nothing said if speaking out is inconvenient, and nothing changed until change has become the only hope of survival.

But the difficulties that have now arisen, as those in control so delicately describe them, are not the result of amazing coincidence, of accident or fate, linking the lives of families in west Belfast, unlucky enough to have fallen prey to Brendan Smyth, with the political and legal careers of Albert Reynolds and Harry Whelehan.

Some of those whose wounds were exposed in UTV's *Counterpoint* programmes spoke of their regret at the way in which their wounding had led to the resignations of the Taoiseach and the president of the High Court.

They didn't say, but they might have, that they showed more human sympathy for the leaders of public life in this State than the State's political and legal systems – and for too long, the clerical authorities – had shown for them.

They might have added that, if this society had been more responsive to their predicament, we wouldn't now be reeling from the effects of a predicament of our own.

We wouldn't be watching Fianna Fáil sweep up the debris of the Smyth affair. Fianna Fáil: our biggest party, which has done more than any other agency, with the exception of the Catholic Church, to shape our lives. Nor would we be listening to the sounds of a cardinal weeping and judges complaining about the dangers that lurk at the unlit crossing where law and politics intersect.

But the Smyth affair would not have been as damaging as it was – to Church, State or law – if these institutions had been less vulnerable: if they'd been more open, more accountable, more democratic and more attuned to the needs and demands of Ireland in the last decade of the

20th century. If they'd been more honest, with us and with themselves.

The problems that have spread through the sluggish channels of our public life are compounded by the determination of those who run them to stay in control. The minimal changes they permit are not meant to lead to the cutting edge of reform, but to swamps of delay and prevarication.

Some Fianna Fáil deputies were obviously confused about the detailed argument over what had or hadn't passed between Mr Reynolds and his colleagues and the attorney generals, Harry Whelehan and Eoghan Fitzsimons.

How was it, they asked, that their leader, who'd escaped the wordy avalanche of the Hamilton Report and managed time and again to soften Labour's querulous cough, now found himself impaled on the finer points of comparison between one (non-political) extradition and another?

Never mind the backbenchers, several members of the Cabinet found it hard to understand.

Brian Cowen gave a roaring display on RTÉ's *Prime Time* before lumbering off to join his colleagues. As he went, the sound of his voice proclaiming Mr Reynolds' statesmanship echoed from coast to coast. "I want to make this point," were Bashful's most memorable words.

It was one of the high points in a week of surrealism which featured, among other things, a Dáil without a government, a civil servant suspended somewhere between Macedonia and Frankfurt – and so unable to shed light on anything – and messengers from the IRA delivering snappy lectures on the dangers of instability.

Some mysteries were not solved. No one has yet convincingly explained how a note from Mr Fitzsimons (about the earlier extradition case) could have been intended by Fianna Fáil ministers for use on Tuesday in defence of Mr Whelehan's appointment, only to be used 24 hours later to justify criticism so serious that it must have contributed heavily to Mr Whelehan's resignation.

And there was an ominous paragraph in Dick Spring's decisive speech on Wednesday in which he said that he had been prepared to accept statements prepared by Mr Reynolds and Máire Geoghegan-Quinn about their being misled by Mr Whelehan – until he discovered that the information had been available before Mr Reynolds delivered his defence and answered questions.

Now I know that, in the last general election, one of Labour's slogans committed the party to putting trust back into politics. But trust has to be earned, and worked on, as Mr Spring himself said in his powerful contribution to the beef tribunal debate.

And, to judge by callers to radio programmes and people interviewed on the streets, Labour has only now begun to earn its passage in this area, restoring the trust that it lost when it surprisingly joined forces with Fianna Fáil. People who voted for change were not amused and they've become even more unhappy of late.

Proinsias de Rossa, whose speeches, like those of Mary Harney, win less attention than they deserve, said during one of the broadcast Dáil sessions this week that people no longer had to wait to hear or read what was happening – they could see for themselves how their leaders performed.

Someone made the point when television cameras were being introduced to the Dáil and Senate chambers that this was a potentially revolutionary development. It was. The cameras show, without fear, favour or partisan gloss, how things are done; who answers and who does not, and who hides behind Sean Treacy's skirt.

There has been a revival of interest in politics that's good for politics but may be dangerous for politicians. The modernisation which the electorate – and circumstances – demand, will be achieved, as in the old Soviet Union, in two ways: by reform and openness. If the two get out of kilter – or fail to match society's changes – the results could be disastrous.

John Bruton warned this week against closing ranks to avoid

change. One of his predecessors, Liam Cosgrave, said in 1970 that Fianna Fáil had suffered so badly in the Arms Crisis that it would take a generation "to weed it out or breed it out".

Mr Reynolds promised openness but did not deliver. His departure has left a bruised party and confused supporters. In the circumstances, Fianna Fáil may feel tempted to close ranks so as to avoid all but the most unavoidable change. It has never really taken the opportunity presented by a period in opposition to recover its strength and look into its own heart. Now is the time to do it.

MARCH 4th, 1995

Re-formed Bertie and the Bishops need a new song sheet

THERE'S A COUNTRY-and-western singer who complains that his get-up-and-go has just got up and went, but I can't (for the life of me) remember who it is.

If anyone out there knows, would they please get in touch, not with me, but with an old group that's re-forming under a new leader. It's called Bertie and the Bishops and it suffers from the same complaint.

When Mr Ahern replaced Albert Reynolds, he promised to bring back the get-up-and-go that had got up and left Fianna Fáil. After a long procession of clerical scandals, Catholic leaders, too, seemed imbued with a firm purpose of amendment. In both quarters, there was talk of a new beginning. No one wanted a repetition of the twin crises that had afflicted public life.

The suggestion that Fianna Fáil in opposition would come under pressure to move to the right was greeted with an emphatic tut. Neither on the North nor on social issues would the party return to the opportunism that had guided it between 1982 and 1987. Or so we were assured.

In the case of the Catholic clergy, the assurances were less clearly defined. Mistakes had been made and were now, somewhat reluctantly, admitted: those whose task it had been to make generations of children feel guilty had been confronted with their own guilt. In a couple of honourable instances, apologies were offered.

Then we were reminded that the ministers and even the leaders of the Catholic Church are only human. Some, indeed, are more human than others, though you're more likely to hear about humanity when they've done what they tell others not to do than when they're telling the others not to do it.

But should it have been all that surprising to find Fianna Fáil shifting uncomfortably from broad agreement with the other parties on Michael Noonan's Information Bill? Even after its participation in the most reforming government of the century? Probably not.

It was at least as predictable as the latest muttering about Articles 2 and 3 of the Constitution, though few had believed Mr Ahern could be so thoughtless in the present climate as to suggest 'A Nation Once Again' as an alternative to the national anthem.

Abortion is not an easy subject for those who, until lately, shied away altogether from discussion of sex and related issues. Like divorce and contraception, it's a subject that can no longer be avoided.

The number of women now going to Britain for abortions stands at more than 4,000 a year. Since the State refuses to allow clinics here – which would be the most sensible and least hypocritical thing to do – the traffic is bound to continue.

This being so, the journeys, the operations and the aftercare should be made as safe as possible. At least, the electorate decided in 1992, information should be available. To argue that information shouldn't include the names and addresses of clinics is humbug and an insult to the intelligence of the electorate.

As David Andrews said, it's the least that should be done and Michael Noonan, who is determined to do it, is criticised right and left – and threatened by the more thuggish fundamentalists – for carrying out the people's wishes. Many share Mr Andrews' view, among them Liz O'Donnell, Liz McManus, Derek McDowell and, I suspect, several members of the Fianna Fáil front bench, Máire Geoghegan-Quinn, Charlie McCreevy and Mary O'Rourke.

Mr Noonan is obliged to prepare and present legislation. The State is not forcing anyone to avail of the service it provides or permits. The bishops may feel obliged to impose rules on their own followers. They have no right at all to bully the rest of us; and, in the light of experience, they should think twice about wading in among the politicians.

No one expects the Catholic Church to change its views on abortion, divorce, homosexuality or contraception because bishops, priests and brothers have had problems with their sexuality. But the fumbling and evasion of Church leaders as they tried to deal with these affairs were plain to be seen.

Yet the three bishops, Brendan Comiskey, John Magee and Michael Murphy, who spoke or issued statements about abortion this week showed no sign of having learned anything from the controversies of the last three years. No question of humanity or understanding now.

Indeed Dr Magee, who said Mr Noonan's Bill "makes provisions which will facilitate citizens in their attempts to procure abortion", went on to warn that the Church attaches "the canonical penalty of excommunication" to the crime of "formal co-operation in an abortion".

In 25 years of violence in the North, during which the Provisional IRA was responsible for some of the most barbaric murders, Dr Magee's colleagues in the hierarchy studiously refrained from issuing such an explicit threat. Excommunication, they decided, would not work.

But when we discuss abortion and related issues, we stand at a crossroads where politics, religion, medicine and law intersect and the woman, who is faced with the choice, is in danger of being left alone while gatherings of men, often middle-aged or elderly, some bound by celibacy, argue the toss.

Intractable complications arise when a master of one discipline strays into another's territory or – as is the way with some bishops and all fundamentalists – someone believes that he has discovered the truth and, come what may, it's his to broadcast and interpret.

The wisest, if not always the smoothest, way to proceed is by the parliamentary route, which is, or should be, more open and accountable than any other. In any event, it's my view that the body which is most accessible and most answerable to the community is best equipped to serve it.

Some people think otherwise. Mr Justice Rory O'Hanlon bypasses not only the Oireachtas but the electorate and appeals directly to God. Legislation of the kind proposed by the Government, he says, is a profanity against God, in which everyone engaged in the exercise is implicated.

And, as a Catholic, he feels that if he remained silent when this was about to happen he would be "betraying a trust God has imposed on me (as on all members of my faith) just as if I had been a judge in Nazi Germany in the 1930s and 1940s and had remained silent when the Jewish Holocaust was being planned and put into effect".

The comparison with the Holocaust is distorted. It makes little of Hitler's campaign of genocide, insults the humane and honourable efforts of Mr Noonan and his colleagues to meet the wishes of the electorate as expressed in the 1992 referendum. And it ignores the women for whom the information is required.

It raises again the question of the way in which judges are appointed and the absence of effective accountability. It suggests, too, an explanation for Dick Spring's cautious attitude to judicial appointments. We are reminded once more of the American system in which prospective members of the Supreme Court appear before congressional committees.

The socio-sexual issues will not go away. Both here and in the United States, abortion is a potent source of anger and condemnation.

Those who so glibly call up the images of Nazism here should look again at the American experience and, with one eye on the militants in their own ranks, remind themselves of the murders which have lately embarrassed fellow fundamentalists in the US.

MARCH 11th, 1995

Deep in the moral maze, someone is digging

WE'VE TAKEN ANOTHER step this week through the strange, closed world of Ireland's moral maze, with its legal twists and constitutional snares and a political hole from which comes the sound of digging: "Fianna Fáil at work."

Bertie Ahern, who started the hole, had taken his stand nearby in the hope of seeing Michael Noonan fall in. Unfortunately for Fianna Fáil, the party's backbenchers took a hand; they undermined Mr Ahern's position and, ignoring their senior colleagues, all but buried his leadership.

It was Mr Noonan who took on the real guardians of the moral maze with his call on deputies to stand by the primacy of the Dáil and their role as legislators: a speech that echoed Des O'Malley's determination (during a debate on contraception in the mid-1980s) to stand by the Republic.

"I call on all deputies," Mr Noonan said, "to reject those who would reach back into the mist of history and try to pressure us with the ghostly weapons of bell, book and candle." On television, he nodded politely in their lordships' direction and continued to insist that his Information Bill was not about abortion.

Quite so. For their part, the bishops acknowledged the politicians' obligations in the light of the latest constitutional amendment, reminded them of the Catholic Church's position, and insisted that the Bill was designed to provide information which would help to procure abortions.

The problem was back in the hands of the politicians, though both the bishops and their allies had made sure from the start that they would not be allowed to tackle it without interference.

The debate, which began with suspicion and mistrust, the stock in trade of fundamentalism, is not over yet. But the current phase is coming to a close as a wrangle about formulas and definitions, the last refuge of those who live by the slogan.

In the early 1980s, fundamentalists suspected that small but determined forces on the left would avail of political instability to insist on the inclusion of abortion in the programme of any government they promised to support. (No left-wing party that I know of had anything of the sort in mind.)

The fundamentalists suspected the left; they still didn't trust the right. They believed that neither Fianna Fáil nor Fine Gael would resist any offer to form a government, whatever the partnership or the conditions on which potential partners insisted.

So the anti-abortionists did precisely what they suspected pro-choice groups of doing: they took advantage of the uncertainty produced by three elections in a row (during 1981 and 1982) and insisted on a referendum which would write a ban on abortion into the Constitution.

The referendum was to serve several purposes. It would mobilise anti-abortion forces who could later be used in other campaigns. It would spike the guns of pro-choice groups who would henceforth have to fight yet another referendum if they wanted to remove the ban.

And, the fundamentalist planners must have thought not only would they teach the mainstream politicians a thing or two about organisation and efficiency, they would give some lackadaisical bishops a lesson in single-mindedness and Catholic orthodoxy.

Securing Garret FitzGerald's agreement to hold the referendum was the first step in their crusade. With Fianna Fáil's support, they were able to dictate the wording, which meant that they set the question for the electorate; and by labelling anyone who made trouble for them as soft on abortion they were able to see many a would-be critic off the pitch.

Their success in the 1983 referendum was daunting and the coalition they welded to achieve it took on the over-enthusiastic proponents of divorce in 1986 with another winning formula.

The punters might fail to be convinced by the bishops with their pale-faced theology; they were bound to be swayed by arguments about the hussy from over the hill and the family farm.

So far so good for the fundamentalists and their determination to have their way with the rest of the electorate. (Those who are opposed to abortion or divorce but who don't attempt to impose their views on everyone else are not by definition in the fundamentalist camp.)

But neither the bishops nor the fundamentalists were as successful with the politicians as they were with the public at large. This will be the third occasion on which a determined Minister in a supportive Government chose to take note of clerical opinion before embarking on an independent course of action.

In 1985, Barry Desmond produced a measure which made contraception widely – though not uniformly – available. In the lifetime of the last Government, Máire Geoghegan-Quinn conformed with the ruling of the European Court of Human Rights by introducing a Bill to decriminalise homosexual acts between consenting adults.

As Mr Noonan was to do, Mr Desmond and Mrs Geoghegan-

Quinn acted quickly and without fuss. The fundamentalists grumbled and public attitudes took time to settle: there were a few sleazy displays of homophobia, and contraceptive supplies are still scarce in some health board areas.

But the world as we knew it remained intact. As in Jim McDaid's case this week, the curse of Cromwell was invoked; but without effect. The electorate did not wreak vengeance on the errant ministers or their parties, and fundamentalism failed to win widespread support.

This week's visit to the moral maze arose directly from the 1983 amendment and its failure to do what the fundamentalists expected of it when the State was confronted with the X case. The idea that you can find a formula which takes care of every case in every circumstance is an illusion.

Those who think otherwise end up countering every legal, constitutional, medical and political argument with a return to first principles, a refusal to compromise and the conviction that everyone else is wrong. The rest of us remember the poignant Turner cartoon of a pregnant youngster confined to an Ireland-shaped camp surrounded by barbed wire.

There was another striking image of the world according to PLAC, SPUC and Youth Defence of late. It was a photograph taken at a Youth Defence demonstration for which some of the women had dressed the part – in cowled habits like the *chador* of their sisters under the *sharia*.

For a woman in the strange closed world of Ireland's moral maze to indulge in sexual activity for any purpose other than reproduction, or indeed to depart in any way from the blessed orthodoxy, is to risk an intimidating range of penalties stretching from lace-curtained disapproval to excommunication (for abortion).

I'm reminded of that respectable and subversive senator, Alexis FitzGerald Snr, who, during one of the apparently endless debates on contraception in the 1970s, reflected on our numerous sexual taboos and said of sex: "I'm past it, but by heavens I'm for it."

Time for a language the people do know

THIS IS A tale of a party which set out in good faith to write a constitution for Ireland of the 1990s and ended deeply frustrated and sadly misunderstood.

The party was the Progressive Democrats. The draft constitution which they produced in January 1988 had occupied two of their leading lawyers, Michael McDowell and Gerard Hogan, for many months.

They'd taken what they considered to be the best of Éamon de Valera's 1937 document, re-examined the work of the committee set up by Seán Lemass in the mid-1960s to review it, and were guided by the modernising spirit of their own reforming leader, Des O'Malley.

Their document had most of the features that a draft constitution for the 1990s ought to have. The language was clear if not eloquent, the approach was more direct than in 1937.

The lines between Church and State were more sharply drawn; they could hardly have been less so. There was a more realistic attitude to Northern Ireland. Unnecessarily complicated passages were trimmed, rewritten or omitted.

The document was launched in the Constitution Room of the Shelbourne Hotel, a venue chosen in symbolic acknowledgment of the debt which the authors – and de Valera – owed to the State's first Constitution, which had been introduced there in 1922.

Initial reactions were encouraging. The authors and the party were praised for recognising the need for change while retaining enough of the de Valera and Free State constitutions to ensure continuity.

The party's annual conference in Cork a few months later changed all that. During the weekend, the document was patiently explained and soberly argued by Mr O'Malley and his colleagues. Most delegates appeared satisfied by the case they made.

A few, however, objected to the omission of de Valera's pious Preamble with its dedication to God and the Holy Trinity; one or two claimed that it looked as if the party meant to drop God from the Constitution.

The leadership which, on the way to Cork, had been more worried about Articles 2 and 3 than about God, was relieved when a resolution criticising this omission was defeated. Somewhere between Mallow and Limerick Junction on the way home, they began to congratulate themselves on a job well done.

At the back of the train, the defenders of the faith licked their wounds and complained like Lily in Joyce's story 'The Dead' about "the men that is nowadays". Little did they know...

The Progressive Democrat train was trundling through the midlands when a fresh RTÉ correspondent introduced them to viewers as the party that was, indeed, bent on taking God out of the Constitution. The description was reinforced next morning by an irreverent piece in this newspaper. Heavier guns manned by Fianna Fáil and the clergy were hauled up to finish the job.

The Progressive Democrats' Constitution for the 1990s was as dead as a doornail by lunchtime.

The trouble was: we needed McDowell and Hogan, and we need T K Whitaker and his expert committee on the Constitution now. How much we needed them was already clear when the 50th anniversary of de Valera's Constitution was marked by a drone of seminars and lectures in 1987.

Judges past and present were wheeled out. Historians, lawyers and journalists threw in their tuppenceworth and stood back to see what the politicians would make of it. The answer was: not much. All of those who favoured change were in opposition. The minority Fianna Fáil Government had other fish to fry, or beef to grill.

What was said then, in 1987, was little different from what had been said for years about the Constitution: roughly, that it was a living document, capable of development and in need of repair. But it could neither be developed nor repaired without Fianna Fáil's agreement and the acquiescence of the Catholic bishops.

Fianna Fáil looked the other way. The bishops smiled. Agreement on change, it seemed, was out of the question. As usual, the tone of the public debate was hushed and solemn – like a conversation among mourners at the back of a church while the coffin was being carried out.

That it was Fianna Fáil's Constitution no one appeared to doubt. But there were few references to the failure of the 1960s review to produce the radical results Lemass had hoped for.

He believed the Constitution should be rewritten every 30 years. All that happened (and then only in 1972) was that the special position of the Catholic Church was removed.

What remains, marginally amended, is a document that presumes to speak to and for the people, but in a language which the people do not know and from a point of view of which most of them are only vaguely aware.

The Preamble still reads: *In the name of the Most Holy Trinity, from Whom is all authority and to Whom, as our final end, all actions both of men and States must be referred,*

We, the people of Éire,

Humbly acknowledging all our obligations to our Divine Lord, Jesus Christ, Who sustained our fathers through centuries of trial,

Gratefully remembering their heroic and unremitting struggle to regain the rightful independence of our Nation...

This sounds more like an extract from a penny catechism than a political declaration, and it's a good deal more humbly unctuous than the text that follows. But what we are for has always been more difficult to declare than what we are against.

There was a story about a crusty elder of the 1960s who barked at his students: "You're agin the bomb, you're anti-apartheid, you're opposed to colonialism and discrimination and censorship. Tell me, what are you bloody well for?"

The answer, of course, was obvious. The trouble with nationalism, on the other hand, is that it tries to pin all responsibility on one, external, source. And, in our case, when you take the anti-Britishness away, there's very little left.

But our past has had little or nothing to do with our constitutional oddities and absurdities. There, responsibility rests with ourselves alone. The confinement of women to the home is taken for granted. The most memorable assertion of children's rights, that the children of the nation should be cherished equally, comes from the 1916 Proclamation, not the Constitution.

Given the inferior roles of women and children and the unassailable rights of the family and private property, we are left with an impression of unbreakable patriarchy. The family is not defined but simply understood in the most limited, conventional sense.

Now is the time for definition and redefinition.

As an editorial in the current issue of the quarterly review *Times Change* suggests, it may even prove possible in a newly defined state for those whose politics is founded on the idea of a republic (a *res publicae*) to "pursue those legitimate objectives of preferring public good over private interest".

As the greatly admired T K Whitaker and his expert colleagues assemble to re-examine the 1937 Constitution, they ought to think, not so much of the political constraints which would have them proceed at the pace of the slowest towards minimal change, but of the exciting possibilities of new generations responding to a new sense of ourselves.

Advisers cry foul in league of grievances

TAX ADVISERS ARE the last people you expect to find in the front competing – slogan for slogan – with Sinn Féin for top spot in the league of grievances.

But that's where they've been and what they've been doing since Ruairí Quinn published his Finance Bill – calling for radical action against what they describe as an informer's charter.

And if you've been bored to sleep by the endless complaints of Gerry Adams and Martin McGuinness, you should listen awhile to Ruairí Quinn's indignant critics, who are equally self-righteous and as convinced as the Sinn Féiners that they know best.

The charter, so-called, is Section 153, which obliges auditors, accountants and solicitors in certain circumstances to report the crime of tax evasion among their corporate clients.

The Law Society, representing the solicitors, makes no bones about its hostility. "The Law Society has advised solicitors not to comply with Section 153 of the Finance Bill 1995 if it is enacted."

The reason for the switch from lawyers to possible lawbreakers is simple. The society has had the advice of two barristers – "top experts on constitutional law" – who have said that, because of the element of self-incrimination, the section is unconstitutional. And that's that.

As for the accountants, day after day their representatives are found insisting – in the press, on radio and television – that Section 153 is not only unconstitutional but unworkable, unnecessary and unjust.

Both groups complain of potential breaches of confidentiality and the lawyers make much of legal professional privilege which, they say, is a fundamental feature of the administration of justice and the rule of law.

Together, solicitors and accountants opened the active phase of their campaign by walking out of a meeting with the Revenue Commissioners and suspending co-operation with them.

Less than a month later, they are in full cry, their language and cry heightened to a degree that would embarrass many a trade union official.

Someone threw in a reference to the KGB. An accountant found this brought to mind "a further analogy of children being encouraged to rat on their parents in the Nazi regime".

RTÉ's *Marketplace* programme made a convenient platform on which to threaten the tax advisers' equivalent of angry voices and stamping feet, a long, hot summer indeed. There were a few clipped contributions from Mr Quinn on film, but there was no attempt at dialogue between the parties.

At the Dáil committee to which the bodies representing solicitors and accountants were invited, Joe Gannon of the Institute of Chartered Accountants, which has 10,900 members, said that Section 153 "will lead to a sub-culture of shady advice and service from inside and outside the State".

And Charlie McCreevy, a member of the committee, was later heard to observe: "I don't think the informer culture is part of the Irish psyche", which was probably meant to support the view that trying to get tax advisers to report offences was pointless anyway.

This is an old story, regularly told when questions are raised about those who do and those who don't pay tax. About the ability of some to exploit the system and the inevitability that others meet the shortfall.

It's about cute hoors and their agents, whether in politics or business, and shady deals where politics and business intersect; where, up to now at least, those who could afford the biggest political contributions and the fattest fees enjoyed every advantage at the expense of the rest.

At the Oireachtas select committee on finance and general affairs,

Tommy Broughan of Labour annoyed the tax advisers by pointing to the scandal of unpaid taxes, claiming that auditors could not be trusted to report evasion and suggesting that some advisers had made evasion their business.

Such claims invariably give rise to argument. But there's no argument about the background to the introduction of Section 153, any more than there is serious doubt about the need to reinforce legally the provisions of the accountants' professional code of practice.

Mr Quinn introduced the section on foot of a promise made by two governments – the present coalition and its Fianna Fáil–Labour predecessor – to act on the recommendations of Mr Justice Liam Hamilton in the Beef Tribunal Report.

The tribunal uncovered systematic tax evasion on a huge scale, as well as systematic fraud in the European Union. It was because a company of auditors knew of the evasion but had not reported it – was not obliged by law to do so – that Mr Quinn chose to make the offence reportable.

Not instantly reportable – time is allowed to consult the client and remedy the matter. Not for every tittle-tattle, as some suggest; there's an initial allowance of £5,000. And it's not a frivolous imposition – tax evasion is a crime.

However, Mr Quinn decided that not only auditors but other accountants and solicitors should be bound by it – a source of particular grievance among the lawyers, who accept there are grounds for including the accountants but object to their own inclusion.

The accountants argue that the events which gave rise to the Beef Tribunal are no more than a bad memory. They suggest that the incidence of tax evasion has declined of late and, as for the involvement of accountants, they have their own way of dealing with errant colleagues.

However, the Revenue Commissioners confirm that the amount of tax outstanding from the self-employed as of May last year stood at

£612 million. And the £260 million yielded by the 1993 tax amnesty did not represent the expected haul of large sums of repatriated hot money, but the revelation of some 38,000 defaulters – most of them on the home front.

As for errant accountants, when Peter Cassells of the Irish Congress of Trade Unions challenged Roger Hussey of the Institute of Chartered Accountants in Ireland to say what action had been taken against them for breach of their own code of practice, Mr Hussey would not say. Mr Hussey is one of many advisers claiming that their objections to informing the Revenue Commissioners about tax evasion by their clients is somehow comparable to the refusal of journalists in certain circumstances to divulge their sources.

There is no comparison between the practices. Journalists protect their sources so that they can inform the public of affairs that might otherwise remain hidden. The disclosure – as in the case of Susan O'Keeffe who appeared before the beef tribunal – contributes to the common good.

The confidentiality on which tax advisers insist is designed to achieve the opposite effect. They protect their clients at a price to ensure that they do not contribute to the common good.

Here they might remember that this is the European week of action on unemployment. And that the Irish National Organisation of the Unemployed is struggling to secure sufficient Government funds so the community employment schemes can retain 7,000 places which will otherwise be lost.

Rich world reluctant to end silence on famine

WHEN THE GOVERNMENT called for suggestions as to how the Famine of the 1840s should be commemorated, the thought must have occurred to many that it ought to be by a policy designed to fight famine now.

The motif was supplied by the President when, at a conference in New York in early summer, she appealed to the international community in terms that linked Ireland's past, the present plight of Somalia and the unforged conscience of the modern world.

Mrs Robinson felt "a profound sense of anger and outrage and, indeed, self-accusation that we are all participants in re-enacting the Great Irish Famine".

"Poverty," she said, "is the companion of hunger. But so is silence. Breaking that silence allows us to see the past, not only in its suffering but in its complexity."

The developed world's reluctance to break its silence now is matched by our own reluctance, over many generations, to face the reality of a famine which, as Mrs Robinson said, was not just the country's history but – for so many – family history.

For the developed world, breaking the silence – admitting the crises of hunger and poverty to primetime television – would be to meet a challenge which calls for more than old rhetoric adapted to new circumstances. It calls for new and maybe domestically unpopular policies.

Here, it has taken a long time to challenge the myths of a famine too often glimpsed as another hazy episode in the history of nationalism.

I still remember a sense of excitement at the publication of Cecil Woodham-Smith's book, not because it succeeded in explaining the causes and consequence of The Great Hunger but because, in the 1940s and 1950s, we were familiar only with a blurred outline and the most simplistic interpretation of events.

It was not until the excellent work of Cormac Ó Gráda began to be published that we were able to see the past not only in its suffering but in its complexity.

Our official version lent itself to the simplistic interpretation against which Dr Ó Gráda warned: blight caused the failure of the potato crop three seasons in a row; since the potato was their only food, people starved or died of the fever; death and emigration halved a population of 8 million in three years.

But, as the official version went, none of this was inevitable. The Irish people produced enough grain to feed themselves – if it had not been taken for rent by the landlords' agents and shipped to England to meet the demands of absentee landlords.

Guilt was firmly nailed to the doors of the Big Houses. The Soupers who gave, or took, soup were also to blame. Worst of all, there was the Government in London with its damned colonial system.

The official version was no more detailed and suggested no greater complexity than that. Its authors would probably have said that it served its purpose. And, as far as it went, it did.

The whole truth – the full complexity – called for more time, energy and curiosity than they were prepared to invest.

Indeed, with a few exceptions, we've learned as much or more about the Famine from plays and playwrights – T C Murray, Gerard Healy, Tom Murphy and Eoghan Harris – than from historians.

Where one might have expected monuments and studies, there was emptiness and silence. For a people given to introspection – our national pastime, according to the anthropologist, Eileen Kane – this was a strange omission.

Was it shame? Or guilt? Or superstition? The fear that, by dwelling on one catastrophe, we risked bringing another down on ourselves.

Because, of course, the Famine of the 1840s was not the first visitation and would not be the last.

Of this, too, the official version had little to say. Twenty years ago in Corca Dhuibhne, I was stopped short by a local historian who pointed out that many of those who went to settle in Springfield, Massachusetts, had left after a famine of the 1870s. But we had heard nothing of famine before or after the 1840s.

Fifty years ago my father spent much of his time, after school, visiting old people to collect the folklore of east Clare. I went with him on his rounds, especially when he met two brothers, Con and Solomon O'Neill, who were in their eighties or early nineties.

They needed only a little coaxing to tell how the fairies of our own Cruaic a' Bharraile had taken revenge on the fairies from the Limerick side by rolling them down the mountain in barrels. They knew all there was to know about holy wells and pattern days. But when they were asked what they knew about the Great Famine – which ended, at most, 15 years before they were born – they would say only that their family had had nothing to do with it.

Yet David Fitzpatrick could write in his achingly beautiful *Oceans of Consolation* (Cork University Press) that the Famine was "to linger longer in Clare than in other counties".

My aunt, whom I asked years later about the old men's reticence, pointed to a field by a stream we knew as the Sandy River and said that people went there to eat the clover and a type of sorrel which grew between the woods and the Shannon.

When I asked who they were she said: "Mountainy people. Poor ould *spailpíns*. They used to find them dead in the ditches."

Poor *spailpíns*. Sean MacReamoinn, in a lecture written four years ago, suggested that here was a reason for the curious absence of popular interest in the Famine: it was the class system which some refused to acknowledge, though it decided who survived and who died of starvation and disease.

Those who died were for the most part the poorest of the poor, landless labourers or *spailpíns*, the tenants of tenant farmers with helpless families and a bare toehold on a few roods and perches of bad land. A discriminatory inheritance system forced them to divide and subdivide what they had.

From a reading of the work which has now been done by Ó Gráda, Fitzpatrick and others, it's clear that the emigrants were those who could afford to go; and there were some who seem not only to have stayed and survived, but to have thrived.

The enemy, as Michael Davitt told the people of Mayo when he founded the Land League little more than 30 years later, was not just the absentee landlords or English landlords, but landlordism and those of whatever nationality or religion who used the system for exploitation.

Davitt, who as a Fenian had spent years in the depths of English jails, organised his first League campaign against a landlord who happened to be a Catholic priest, in Irishtown, Co. Mayo.

He saw through the vainglorious folly of some erstwhile comrades in physical-force groups and recognised the damage inflicted on the cause of a majority of the Irish people by others.

He suffered imprisonment and the effects of famine and emigration. But he came to know, as we are beginning to learn, that it's better to respond to the complexity of life than to pretend that it's all plain sailing. The commemoration of the Famine should not be simple.

Divorce defeat would spur the cultural defenders to intervene again

IT'S NOT TRUE that whatever happens on Friday nothing will change. It would be foolish to campaign for divorce only to claim when the day was done that it didn't matter.

And the result of a vote against the Government's proposal is unlikely to be confined to retaining the constitutional ban. Those who have worked so hard to prevent change are not going to stop there.

Many of these cultural defenders have already campaigned on every socio-sexual issue put to the electorate since 1983 and success now would encourage them to intervene again on abortion, censorship, euthanasia.

In the present campaign, they agree with their opponents on one crucial point. This is not simply about the right to remarry. It's about our society, how we see ourselves and each other. And, those who favour change will add, it's about our regard for minorities.

As on many other political issues which have come to be decided of late, it's also about trust. To write conditions for divorce into the Constitution is to acknowledge a lack of trust in politicians.

But there is a sense in which what's at issue here is both wider and deeper than that, it's trust in the maturity, responsibility and even the religious convictions of the public at large.

Many opponents of divorce have already shown their mistrust, not only of politicians but of the Supreme Court and the bishops.

Now they argue that Catholics generally are so feebly or unreliably committed to the vows they make during the marriage ceremony that the State must be on hand to enforce them.

People who claim they are able to fathom the mysterious depths of Church nullity and to tell the difference between it and secular divorce expect us to believe that their marriages are undermined by the mere existence of divorce.

This is like saying that the existence of coronary units encourages heart attacks. And as for the canonical procedures, even William Binchy admitted this week to being baffled by a question about Pauline privilege.

The Government must meet the problems of real lives, not the cardboard cutouts designed by theologians or lawyers. In the end, the people must be neither the puppets of fundamentalists, lay or clerical, nor cowed and bullied into line by Youth Defence.

The decision on the right to remarry cannot be isolated from the rest of our affairs, social, economic and political. Which is why it were best decided by the electorate in partnership with the leaders we choose to handle the rest of our affairs.

Unfortunately, it's being decided in a welter of hysteria stirred by groups, some of uncertain provenance, bound obsessively to a series of single issues.

Some opponents of divorce object to being called fundamentalists. "Cultural defenders" is a term which seems to cover all of them, stretching from Professor Binchy to Bishop Thomas Flynn, and from Nora Bennis to Youth Defence, Christian Solidarity and back.

The term "cultural defenders" was devised by the political scientist Tom Garvin to describe those who took it upon themselves to defend our traditional way of life against real or imagined attack. After they'd defined tradition and identified the attackers, of course.

In the present referendum, most of them march under Anti-Divorce or No Divorce banners in separate but parallel campaigns, occasionally critical of each other but united in criticism of the bishops, with whom they share their blue-eyed certainty and an immediate objective.

At some crossroads, they all meet, as when they refuse to

distinguish between breakdown and divorce or argue with passionate intensity that, if it's introduced here, divorce will follow the headlong example set by Britain and the United States.

The proponents of divorce deny this. Some say the pattern more likely to be followed is that of two Catholic countries, France and Italy. It seems unlikely though not as outlandish as the comparison with Britain and the US.

It's much more likely that, if the people of this State vote for the right to remarry, what we will have will not be a form of divorce that follows British, mainland European or American lines. It will be like everything else about us, peculiarly Irish.

This is neither a criticism, appealing to the inferiority complex of some, nor a boast in search of nationalist applause from others. It's a matter of fact. We are, by the same token, fair to middling Europeans not in imitation of anyone else, aspiring Germans but in our own way.

The cultural defenders claim to have a high regard for a way of life which they first define and then defend as they see fit.

But it's their way of life, not that of the public at large. It's exclusive, walled in, limited and unchanging.

They look upon it as their property and, in a sense, it is. It is as often as not the product of their imagination, and they want others to conform to it. It has faults and failings which, like our more joyful characteristics, are indeed our own.

They call them "traditional", which is a powerful defence in a community which has a high regard for tradition. But as the great Sydney Smith noted in the 18th century, the appeal to tradition is used as often to justify some skulduggery of the present as to honour some feature of the past.

The cultural defenders would have us believe that marital breakdown is not in the Irish tradition. It's something, they say, that our forefathers did not do. And if by chance we fall, the remedy is to be found inside marriage dead or alive, not in its dissolution.

But for those who grew up in a small town or a country place, where nothing remains hidden for long, it's impossible to ignore or forget those marriages which must have set out with hope and ended in sad or poisonous failure.

I've heard the idea that people can lead separate lives under one roof scorned by some as a convenient legal fiction. But how vividly I remember an old couple who passed our house in Clare four times a week going to and from town on Saturdays, to and from Mass on Sundays.

The poor man always walked a few yards ahead of his poorer wife. They sometimes paused to talk to us and we watched to see if they would talk to each other. They never did. It wasn't the only example of a dead marriage in our parish, simply the most obvious.

Given the extent to which caste and class influenced relations between men and women, the matches made for imposed-on couples and the way in which women were traded against dowries of land or money, it was a wonder that more marriages didn't end badly.

The reason they didn't had more to do with the social stigma of failure than religious conviction. How many couples were imprisoned in marriage? How many condemned to a life in which they made each other pay for failure?

This is the legacy that has informed our debate, which has not been helped by Dr Flynn's attempt to terrify people any more than by Ruairí Quinn's insult to Mr Binchy.

What we have on Friday is an opportunity to break free. I hope we take it.

Past holds no answers for terror of today

AN AMERICAN JOURNALIST called Lincoln Steffens, who visited the Soviet Union in 1919, recorded his impression in a memorable sentence: "I have seen the future and it works."

If only it had been, not just memorable, but true.

I remembered the phrase when some of those commenting on crime in Ireland in the 1990s took to citing the 1950s as years of certainty and security.

Clearly, another case of wishful thinking: we have seen the past and it didn't work either.

And, as I write, these words, which were intended to convey the folly of trying to recreate the conditions of 49 years ago, take on a more ominous meaning.

Reports from London confirm an IRA bombing at Canary Wharf, though with what authority is still unclear.

So much has been invested in the movement towards peace by politicians in Ireland, Britain and the US. So many hopes have been raised among the people of Northern Ireland that it would be tragic if it were so cruelly halted now.

But if the reported IRA statement is genuine and the ceasefire which began 18 months ago has indeed been broken, then the task of those who were so hesitantly circling each other in the search for a political settlement becomes not just urgent but desperate.

As I listen, politicians are still clinging to the hope that Sinn Féin, at least, has not abandoned the peace process. If this is the case, then an essential link in the process will have been saved.

If not, our concerns with violence on a local scale and comparisons with the 1950s will prove insignificant. As it is, all it takes to put a superficial shine on the 1950s is a rub of nostalgia.

But it's hard to understand how anyone who lived through those years – unlike the young fogeys who simply wished they had – can pine for their return.

True, it was a decade in which authority was unquestioned and property respected, the streets were safe and, if people were poor, at least they knew their place.

That place, as a rule, was England. It was the place, not only for the poor and jobless, but for anyone who questioned authority or fell foul of the law.

Many a defendant was given the benefit of the doubt on the promise that he'd head straight for the train and boat and a berth with the brother in Kilburn. We exported our crime just as we exported unwanted pregnancies or anything else that was better out of sight and out of mind.

There were side effects, of course. The population fell drastically. Between 1951 and 1961 around 410,000 people went, mostly to England. Seán Lemass in opposition claimed the rate was higher.

(When Fianna Fáil was in power, we in the *Irish Press* didn't mention emigration at all. As Joe Walsh said in the Dáil during the week, Fianna Fáil doesn't stand for evasion.)

Emigration not only kept the crime rate down, it sapped the energy of towns, villages and country places, inspired such books as *The Vanishing Irish* and left a particularly compliant crew in charge where the bulk of the population was made up of the very young and the old.

But those who say that this is a fearful society – having done their best to make it so – are wrong to suggest a contrast with the 1950s; at least as wrong as in their wild comparisons with other countries.

When the novelist Deirdre Purcell was asked lately on RTÉ about the atmosphere of the early 1960s when she was growing up, she said the pervasive feeling was one of fear.

She recalled being afraid of people in authority, "afraid of everybody".

Just so. The 1950s and early 1960s, during which the potentially troublesome part of the population was shipped overseas, was a period in which many who remained were cowed or beaten into submission.

My father, a teacher, often warned youngsters that they'd end up in an industrial school. He'd taught in such a school when he first qualified and, ever afterwards, loathed the Brothers who ran the place with appalling brutality.

In our secondary school some of the teachers – priests in this case – decided that the way to wake people up on raw mornings was to beat the daylights out of them with leather straps and wooden towel rollers. I suppose they thought that, in a class of 30, they were bound to hit someone who deserved it.

Deirdre Purcell was right: an air of casual and unremitting violence pervaded the 1950s. These were the years when the industrial schools, orphanages and laundries, which have lately been exposed, were not just functioning, but considered to be performing a valuable public service.

For some odd reason – perhaps because so many of the poor had gone – the illusion that Ireland was a classless society gained ground at the time. Lemass was quoted saying so in the London *Times*.

No one would dream of pretending that ours was a classless society now: the people who were once safely dispatched on the *Princess Maud* or locked behind orphanage doors are no longer out of sight and off our consciences.

Some are on our doorsteps, on the perimeters of cities and towns; living in areas of cheap local authority housing often designed, it would appear, to resemble the camps of the migrant poor in some of the major cities of southern Europe.

But political attention is focused on poverty and the risks it carries only when a bout of violence occurs and then, as often as not, the official reaction – not to mention that of wild-eyed commentators – is to reach for old institutional remedies and convenient scapegoats.

Then reason takes flight and the air is thick with screams of fear and anger. Anyone who is not already afraid must begin to worry, and futile rage is directed at a Minister who cannot even get a hearing for the facts.

If the Minister is the first, most obvious scapegoat, Travellers come next – Ireland's version of the racist card, played by some politicians for convenience and, more shamefully, by journalists and broadcasters.

The pattern is familiar. Because the gardaí say they suspect Travellers are involved in some attacks, some reporters and commentators seek links between Travellers and all other violent events, including murders.

The case for the connection is made whether the evidence supports it or not, and at present the evidence is thin: most of the highly publicised murders of late appear to have differed little from the commonplace.

AUGUST 17th, 1996

The label and slogan schools of debate

ONE OF OUR favourite pastimes is asking each other how we stand and before anyone has time to answer, throwing in our own tuppenceworth, with which all right-thinking citizens are expected to agree.

The opinion leaders of other countries retreat to quiet places, or steal away, as the saying goes, to spend more time with their families. They do things differently here.

Our talkers, and some of our thinkers, descend in summer swarms on familiar venues, not for rest and contemplation but to continue the arguments they'd left unfinished in Dublin, Cork and Belfast. From the

MacGill School in Glenties to the Merriman in Ennistymon, with detours to Carnlough for Hewitt, Mayo for Humbert and Avondale for Parnell, the motto is we must be talking to ourselves.

To ourselves, about ourselves, often for our ears only. Rarely if ever with clear and unequivocal results.

Benedict Kiely, a masterly storyteller, novelist and singer of ballads, worked for the *Irish Independent* when newspapers were better written and the *Irish Independent* was more widely read.

Kiely, who was employed to write leading articles, was given unmistakable instructions. His subjects were the co-operative movement and godless Russia.

He could write more or less as he pleased, bearing in mind, of course, that the co-operative movement was a good thing and godless Russia was not. The one thing he must not do, in any circumstance, was to reach a conclusion.

However they came to hear of it, our present leaders of opinion – politicians, journalists, academics, Jacks and Jills of all trades – seem to have taken this old Abbey Street precaution to heart. They can give or take extreme views. Indeed, there's nothing they like better than to watch opponents from opposite camps prove that they are, beyond doubt, irreconcilable.

Someone of the There's-Ireland-For-You school announces nothing in the country works and that we're living in what amounts to the Fawlty Towers of western Europe. Everyone immediately rushes off in search of some hothead of the Wake-Up-Lads-Or-Ye'll-Miss-The-Insult school. And the two are set at each other's throats.

Names and labels are traded, high horses mounted, dollops of umbrage taken and good faith is called into question all round. There are a few cantankerous letters in *The Irish Times*.

Then, after five days of angry phone calls to RTÉ, a half-dozen attacks on nationalists in the *Sunday Independent* and a dozen on lefties in the *Sunday Business Post*, normal service is resumed.

Needless to say, no real damage has been done. No one has said anything for which he or she might be called to account later. No conclusions have been reached.

Without labels, slogans and violent partisanship, controversy is all but impossible. (Someone I knew used to accuse people of being drunk and refusing to fight.)

There was poor Emily O'Reilly on *Saturday View* last week, doing her best to drum up a programme that would do justice to the clichés used in advance of the weekend in Derry.

The people assembled in the studio were civilians: two women and two men, two Protestants and two Catholics, whose qualifications for participation were that they worked and lived in Derry. They were neither politicians nor paramilitaries, though one of the four was in the Women's Coalition and another said he had voted for the coalition in the assembly elections.

None of them justified provocation or sounded as though they would have refused to condemn – let alone order – the smashing to pulp of some frightened youngster's hands and legs.

They were proud of Derry's achievements without for a moment forgetting its failures. They were highly critical of the media for their contributions to the city's fears for the weekend.

And while they recognised the reasons for Protestants leaving the Foyle's west bank since the 1960s, and for Catholic anger in the aftermath of Drumcree, they were reluctant to apportion blame and flatly refused to be partisan.

The presenter tried hard to liven things up. The participants refused to be livened up in the way in which politicians or the representatives of paramilitaries might have been. One said he was beginning to think he'd wandered into the wrong studio. All four acknowledged there were issues on which they were unwilling or unable to comment.

Halfway through the programme, the thought occurred to me

that it was now impossible to tell who was Catholic and who was Protestant. What they had to say about the remoteness and staleness of politics or the alienation of young people, Protestant or Catholic, was suddenly more important than the tribal labels that might have been stuck on the speakers.

This set me thinking of a television programme about pilgrims of different denominations which I'd watched a few years ago with my favourite aunt in our family home in Clare. I've tried but failed to find out who made it. Memory tells me it was the work of an independent company, Iskra, and the admirable Gerry Gregg, but I can't be sure.

The film followed two groups, one Catholic, one Protestant, on their journeys to church or shrine. As they travelled they sang or listened to hymns and spoke of their lives and beliefs while the camera moved slowly from homely face to face.

The faces and the countryside through which they moved were so familiar that my aunt might have been aboard one of those buses, and the road they travelled might well have been ours.

But I soon forgot which group was which and turned to my aunt for enlightenment. She'd spent the first half of her life praying for godless Russia's conversion and the second half praying for mine. If anyone could tell the difference, she could.

She couldn't. She said that, if I cast my mind back, I would remember that when we went on pilgrimage they left the labels on the buses.

Nowadays I prefer things without labels, which is one of the reasons I've begun to enjoy the report of the Constitution Review Group, headed by T K Whitaker. The report covers almost 450 pages, and related papers fill over 200. It sounds heavy and, in one sense, it is: you would have to enlist the help of a small pony or a big dog to carry it.

But it's elegantly written and splendidly laid out. It makes its case for a constitution to meet the needs of the new century without throwing cold water on de Valera's document of the 1930s.

For some unexplained reason, the Government issued the report in a hurry in early July. In doing so, the Coalition seems, at first sight, to have failed to do justice to the work of a thoughtful group which, for the most part, is unafraid of conclusions.

AUGUST 31st, 1996

Odd political bedfellows stand by the memory of King Canute

WHAT, I ASK you, does the English Marxist academic, Prof Terry Eagleton, have in common with the Catholic Archbishop of Cashel, Dr Dermot Clifford?

And the answer is: much more than you might think. For one thing, they are opposed to the modernisation of Irish society – at least as it has been proceeding to date.

In the professor's eyes, the fault lies with revisionism. To the archbishop, modernisation means movement towards the separation of Church and State.

Both sound as if they'd have preferred life here to remain as it was over a quarter of a century ago. Before we joined the Common Market and, to use Eagleton's term, became Eurocentric.

Life was simple then. Nationalism seemed to have escaped, avoided or ignored the questions raised by the 50th anniversary of the Easter Rising. The Irish Catholic Church had survived the Second Vatican Council.

We'd been assured by the familiar leaders of Church and State: our small world was safe, at least as long as we resisted the temptation to lift the green curtain that surrounded us.

We were a million miles from the world of the 1990s in which Ireland holds – and capably handles – the presidency of the European

Union and the hierarchy reels from the echoes of fleeing bishops, guilty priests and a lost referendum.

No one would have believed you, a quarter of a century ago, if you'd told them that, in the summer of 1996, the Republic would watch with rapt attention the internal struggles of loyalist paramilitaries, knowing that what happened was bound to affect everyone on this island.

Nor would anyone have guessed that changed circumstances would make political bedfellows of a left-wing English academic and an ultra-conservative Irish archbishop, both prepared to stand by their principles and the memory of King Canute.

Terry Eagleton has a way with words, which is the least that might be expected of a professor of English literature at the University of Oxford. He also has a deep interest in Irish affairs, as he showed by turning up to lecture on 'The Ideology of Irish Studies' at the opening session of this year's Desmond Greaves Summer School.

The professor's theme is revisionism and revisionists. He can't stand them. Deconstructing Irish nationalism, he argues, is fashionable and, with any luck, will get you a job.

What d'ye intend to do with yourself now, son – since you got the five honours in the Leaving Cert?

Oh, I'm going into industry, Da – the deconstruction industry. Mr Eagleton says there's plenty of jobs in it.

"Deconstructing liberal humanism or postmodern pluralism will probably not [get you a job], but it's a mite more original," says the professor.

Indeed it is. And I'm sure the archbishop would agree. Some commentators who were on his side in the debate on divorce keep resurfacing to complain that liberals aren't as liberal as they ought to be.

But is Prof Eagleton the man to make the case? It's hard to say, because it's often hard to tell what point he's making. Or whether what he says can be taken for praise or blame.

Of course, revisionists are always grousing about the misconceived nature of the title. And they're right. "It is," he agrees, "too vague, sloppy a term, a kind of generalised swearing which among other faults covers too many things."

Then, having pointed to the elephant trap, off he goes and falls into it, laying about him with every bit of generalised swearing and every slab of jargon he can lay his hands on.

Take this:

> "The greatest enterprise of historio-graphical revisionism in Ireland was surely the nationalist one, which took the official imperial narrative and rewrote it with breathtaking boldness from below, with all of the courageous imagining, false continuism, Manichean ethics, historical truth and triumphalist teleology that that entailed."

And this:

> "Liberal humanism... tends to be rather sceptical of the political, as our rulers can often afford to be, whereas postmodernism is less sceptical than selective about politics, enthused by gender, ethnicity and post-colonialism but distinctly cool about class struggle, material production and the International Monetary Fund."

I offered the professor's script to friends, colleagues and relatives who, unlike me, had had the benefit of what we used to call higher education. They couldn't make more sense of it.

Of the general drift there seemed to be no doubt: without a Marxist revolution in the wider world, there would be no great change. But most of the professor's message was smothered in thickets of jargon.

He is, however, against abandoning tradition and under this heading includes "a suspicion of the success ethic and respect for a Church without which millions of Irishmen and women would never have been nursed, educated and cared for".

"How utterly non-pluralist," he commented, "to imagine that one could simply *choose* [Eagleton's emphasis] here. Why are the liberal pluralists so zealously one-sided about these matters?"

The question was naive, almost as naive as it was bizarre to wrap a message about the need for class politics in layers of academic gobbledegook.

That other defender of tradition, Dr Clifford, and his colleague, Father Maurice Dooley, a professor of canon law at St Patrick's College in Thurles, might have told Mr Eagleton a thing or two about the nature of debate in Ireland.

Dr Clifford, you may recall, was one of those who argued most forcefully against divorce in last year's referendum – so forcefully indeed that he claimed, among other things, that divorcees were more likely than others to have road accidents.

One of the pieces of legislation introduced to meet the concern of those who worried about the state of marriage generally was the Family Law Act, obliging couples to give three months' notice of their intention to marry.

The act became effective at the beginning of August. Dr Clifford promptly sent a message – with guidelines written by Father Dooley – to priests in his archdiocese.

It said the act was contrary to Canon Law and that, even where a court exemption had not been obtained, the priests should go ahead with the marriage; the couple could seek the civil validation later.

In a comment reported by Nuala Haughey in this newspaper, Father Dooley said the legal technicalities of the new law made it "entirely purposeless and stupid". When politicians criticised Cashel's approach, Dr Clifford went on radio to explain.

The intention, he said, with the plausible air of someone who'd been asked for advice about the catering, was to help those who came from outside to marry here. Myles Dungan dutifully deferred to the archbishop.

Less than an hour later, Father Dooley was on RTÉ's tea-time television news repeating his views and adding that the Family Law Act was unconstitutional.

Eagleton needn't worry: Rome rules in Tipperary.

NOVEMBER 2nd, 1996

Libel trial coverage gets lost in the past

WE WERE ONCE a notoriously introspective people, given to examining the national conscience at every hand's turn.

We haven't yet kicked the habit, but it now takes an event of some importance to set us talking about how we see ourselves.

The opening of Teilifís na Gaeilge on Thursday night was such an event. The Reynolds libel trial in London, which is likely to end next week, is another.

The opening of the television station challenges us to come clean about a murky past in which the Irish language was used to exclude some people and to provide others with a path to power.

It also invites us to look ahead, to the place that Irish will have 10, 20 or 50 years from now, in a hostile environment in which survival – let alone growth – cannot be guaranteed.

The Reynolds case or, to be more precise, its coverage here, reminds us of a time we should have put behind us, when every contact with England or the English set us mulling over old grievances and the 800 years of oppression.

To some who have been in London to write or broadcast on the proceedings in the High Court it is as if, with his libel action against *The Sunday Times*, Albert Reynolds is not only looking for massive damages, but carrying on the fight for Irish freedom by legal means.

So we have reporters who ought to know better comparing the court room and its occupants to an Ealing comedy, as though the whole show were put on for their benefit.

The judge and lawyers, they say, have come straight from central casting; none of them can pronounce Ceann Comhairle.

When Emily O'Reilly discovers that there's an all-English jury, it seems the cards are stacked against us. (In my day, the juries were always half Hungarian.)

In *The Irish Times*, Mr Reynolds is compared to Parnell. And for a while it looks as if the Casement diaries, or the Pigot forgeries, are about to be produced from some lawyer's carrier bag.

But all *The Sunday Times* can run to is a basket of criticism from the Irish papers which Mr Reynolds, the most litigious leader in modern politics, says he hasn't read.

If the criticism of Mr Reynolds in the Irish papers was ignored by the former Taoiseach and his cheerleaders, the criticism of Willie O'Dea by James Price QC was not.

Mr O'Dea, you may remember, exercised his forensic skills on the witnesses appearing before the Dáil committee which investigated the collapse of the Fianna Fáil–Labour Government.

Well, Mr Justice French in the High Court in London said he couldn't understand him and Mr Price, who appears for *The Sunday Times*, giddily suggested elocution lessons.

It was a foolish – patronising – suggestion, and Mr Price duly issued a statement in which he apologised for it.

But not before Jim Kemmy had rumbled to Mr O'Dea's defence, supported by a squad of commentators, eager to share in the insult.

For a moment all ears tuned to Limerick: the city has more accents than rugby clubs, and the dividing lines mark boundaries of class and sport.

(Its favourite rugby song, 'There is an Isle', wasn't written by a Limerick writer or about Limerick. But then 'Faith of our Fathers', now top of the pops, wasn't written by an Irishman or about Ireland.)

Jim listed local lads made good – Richard Harris, Terry Wogan and David Hanly, all with clear accents – and the commentators threw in their tuppenceworth for Willie, the man in the gap.

Both Joe Duffy, on RTÉ, and Jonathan Philbin-Bowman, in the *Sunday Independent*, seem to have spoken to those on Mr Reynolds' side before reporting on the decision of *The Sunday Times* not to call a witness, Fergus Finlay.

"Reynolds Roasts Spring's Chicken" was the heading on Philbin-Bowman's piece in which he wrote of Mr Finlay: "He was 'chicken', a beaming Reynolds said outside, suggesting that, after watching the roasting of Alan Ruddock (former Irish editor of *The Sunday Times*), the Chicken Finlay couldn't take it."

Duffy, said by Philbin-Bowman to have turned into the "Gary O'Toole of jurisprudence during this trial", was only slightly less dismissive on RTÉ.

In the *Sunday Independent*'s stablemate, *The Sunday Tribune*, Helen Callanan wrote:

"Regardless of what anyone thinks of the former Taoiseach, friends and adversaries alike squirmed at the thought of Finlay having volunteered to assist an Australian/British/American media magnate's case against an Irishman in a British court."

There you have it: while some representatives of the Irish media reach for their green flags, others have eyes on a different target, the international media magnate, Rupert Murdoch, who owns *The Sunday Times*.

Do they forget that their own employer is also a media magnate with interests in Britain, South Africa, Australia, New Zealand and the United States (though his US interests are in a different industry)?

Do they not recognise a trace of *Times'* cynicism in their own publications?

The *Sunday Independent* last week carried an excellent article on the trial by Gene Kerrigan; *The Sunday Tribune* had an equally well-made piece by Ann Marie Hourihane.

The Sunday Times, which printed different reports on the Fianna Fáil–Labour collapse in its British and Irish editions, may not be the only paper which tries to have it both ways.

And doesn't anyone consider it important to tell the truth, whatever the nationality of the parties contesting the case?

The aggressive environment dominated by the O'Reillys and the Murdochs is the one in which Teilifís na Gaeilge must survive, and I wish it – and the new Irish-language newspaper, *Foinse* – success.

I've had it in my mind for some time to pay a journalistic tribute to Radio na Gaeltachta and to such RTÉ programmes as *Cúrsaí* and *An Nuacht*.

It's easy to forget how Irish music grew and flourished from the seeds sown by Seán Ó Riada, Sean MacReamoinn, Seamus Ennis and Ciarán MacMathúna with the help of the new medium, radio.

In a more hostile climate, let's hope that Cathal Goan and his young team enjoy a vigorous and argumentative life. Listeners to radio will still find stimulation in *Seo Beo an tSathairn* and quiet pleasure in Liam Mac Con Iomaire's *Leagan Cainte*.

Having zero tolerance for importing a buzz phrase to Co. Kerry

ONE OF THE great nuisances of our time is the fellow who has picked up all the buzz words but has only the haziest idea of their meaning.

It's not easy to see where he's coming from, never mind what he's getting at. Now, if only he'd take something very heavy on board before plunging through the nearest window of opportunity onto the rusty remains of a hidden agenda...

And while he's running it past us, on his way to (or from) the bottom line, could he be persuaded to take his version of zero tolerance with him?

Zero tolerance is a snappy phrase, imported for electoral purposes by our longest-winded politician, John O'Donoghue. Straight from New York to Cahirciveen.

It was instantly adopted by every pub bore and chattering wiseacre who'd revelled in the old news that the country was going to the dogs. For decades.

What it meant depended on the speaker and the audience. It was capable of many interpretations by angry citizens, depending on how angry they were and with whom.

Drug dealers and addicts certainly. Burglars and car thieves, of course. Young people hanging around street corners, probably. Beggars, if deemed aggressive.

Naturally, there were limits. Zero tolerance, yes. But not for traffic offences. Not double yellow lines. And, of course, the guards should get tough but not by stopping and questioning right-thinking people in their own areas.

But those who make it their business to phone chat shows on such issues – and those whose business it is to chat back – know well what they mean by zero tolerance and whom they think the guards should be after.

This is class warfare being advocated by people who would have us believe that class warfare is a thing of the past. Zero tolerance meant something to the people of New York: huge increases in the police force, the prison population and the public service pay bill, for a start.

But, as Dr Paul O'Mahony, the author of *Criminal Chaos: Seven Crises in Irish Criminal Justice*, wrote in this newspaper a fortnight ago: "Zero tolerance has been oversold on claims that its introduction... led directly to substantial reduction in serious crime and safer streets."

Is there a danger of its being oversold here? The Garda Commissioner, Pat Byrne, seems to think so. He called it a lovely, catchy idea, in a tone suggesting caution: "Let's debate exactly what we want." George Maybury was equally cautious when he spoke to the Association of Garda Sergeants and Inspectors: "Zero tolerance is an absolute concept. There is no room for discretion."

Con Donoghue of the Garda Juvenile Liaison Scheme, addressing a conference on childcare, warned of the particularly serious effect on the children now being helped by the scheme.

Almost 90 per cent of those cautioned under the scheme stayed out of trouble. Under a regime of zero tolerance, they would be prosecuted.

Tom O'Malley, a lecturer in law, spoke at the same conference of the growing public appetite for punishment and a vastly reduced tolerance of wrongdoing by children. It wasn't easy for any western government to strike a balance between control and welfare in juvenile justice policy, he said.

Given its decision on bail, the slow passage of the Children's Bill and the tardy implementation of other protective measures, I'm not at all sure the coalition would resist the temptation to go for control.

Crime threatens to loom large in the general election. The public appetite for punishment, whipped up by the media, is growing dangerously. As a recent *Irish Times*/MRBI poll showed, fear of crime is stirred, both by politicians and media, even where the threat and the experience of crime are least.

Zero tolerance is already practised where local communities have learned the barbaric lessons of the paramilitaries; where gangsterism, intimidation and mob rule masquerade as concern for morality or law and order.

We've seen the most extreme examples of this deadly parade in the deaths of Josie Dwyer and David Templeton, one because of an old addiction, the other for no better reason than that a wretched newspaper pointed a hypocritical finger at him.

Finger-pointing has been Eamon Dunphy's stock-in-trade at the *Sunday Independent*, but he seems to have turned over a new leaf lately, if his *Last Word* interview with Martin McGuinness on Radio Ireland is anything to go by.

In about 40 minutes, the only finger pointed was at a listener who called to say that Dunphy was giving McGuinness a very easy time. "What do you expect me to do, John?" Dunphy enquired. "Head-butt him?"

Not exactly, but he might have asked a few hard questions. As it was, he and McGuinness sounded like Pat Kenny and Danny Morrison, only more so.

"Martin, the difficulties of calling a ceasefire for the republican movement... It's a very, very difficult thing to do. What are the difficulties in calling it?"

"Well," said Martin, "there was a psychological difficulty..." But you could sense that some of Dunphy's insights floored McGuinness. As when he suggested that, "The truth of the matter, Martin, is that you have decided – you and your generation of republicans – violence as an answer is futile."

"Well," said Martin again, "what we have here within Sinn Féin is…" And we were off on a tour of South Africa, the Middle East and Hume–Adams.

In 1994, the task had been to convince the IRA that John Hume and Albert Reynolds were "virtually guaranteeing that within a few short months, inclusive peace negotiations about the future of the island would be up and running".

Ireland's leading republican, as he'd called McGuinness at the beginning, had already hinted at the promises that had prompted the ceasefire.

What were they?

Dunphy didn't ask, skipping ahead to what he believed was the heart of the matter: "We come to the kernel. And the kernel is, this was a repressive State…"

"It still is," said McGuinness.

Dunphy ploughed on. "And there was a violent response from the people on the streets. That response hurt and maimed and was terrible in its consequence. Now you have to get back and retrieve that ground and be trusted.

"Now, the people most exposed, you could argue, would be the unionists. I've spoken to friends of mine in Derry – middle-class people – and during the period of the ceasefire, they came to the conclusion that the loyalist people are bigots at heart. The institutions there are beyond reform."

Did the thought cross Martin's mind, too?

It didn't, but by now it probably didn't matter: the interviewer was interviewing himself.

Dunphy summarised what he thought was the Provos' stance: "We are prepared and have been prepared to reflect, reconsider and review our position. On that basis we are willing to do a deal, but if you don't do a deal we are going back to war. That's it, isn't it?"

"That's not my position," said McGuinness.

Dunphy tried again later: "Effectively you are willing to say the IRA ceases to exist if we can have a reformed Northern state."

"Oh, no," said McGuinness. This was Dunphy's Damascus, not his.

Dunphy, carrying on regardless, wondered how McGuinness got on with the unionists: "I frequently see you on television with these people. Do you talk to them?"

"They don't do programmes with us," said McGuinness.

But his political ambition was modest, which impressed Dunphy. "Absolutely. One of the reasons why you are so respected is that you live in a nice, small house and live a working-class life."

JULY 26th, 1997

A terrible symmetry in the life of a tragic triple killer

BRENDAN O'DONNELL'S LIFE was destroyed as surely as he, in turn, destroyed the life of Liam Riney in the woods near Lough Derg in the summer of 1994.

And O'Donnell's destruction began by all accounts when he was little older than the three year old he shot, for no apparent reason, and laid beside his mother's body in Cregg Wood.

It was part of a terrible symmetry of events and circumstance: as a boy often in trouble with his father, O'Donnell had gone to lie on his own mother's grave, a few miles away in Whitegate.

The tragedy bound Liam Riney's mother, Imelda, to her killer, too: she with her dream of the lake and the country around it; O'Donnell with his childhood memories of a place poisoned with violence and fear. And Father Joe Walsh, a man devoted to kinder ways, like Imelda Riney, paid the price of trying to help where detention centres of one kind or another and prison had failed.

It may be that by the time Imelda Riney and Father Joe Walsh arrived in that corner of east Clare and south Galway, which stretches from Whitegate to Woodford, the part that O'Donnell bitterly called home, he was beyond reform.

At his trial, there was disagreement about his mental condition. The expert witnesses were evenly divided; only two of the 12 jurors favoured a finding of guilty but insane. He was found guilty of murder.

Art O'Connor, consultant psychiatrist at the Central Mental Hospital, summed up the question and the answer on RTÉ Radio's *Morning Ireland* yesterday. Was it a case of madness or badness?

"We are talking about badness," he said, pointing out that insanity was a legal concept: what had to be decided was whether someone knew what he was doing and whether he knew that it was wrong.

He also proposed a changed attitude to offenders:

"In the past we've focused on the rights of offenders. This has recently shifted to the protection of others... In the past we have been too concerned with the rights of violent people."

So Brendan O'Donnell was sent to prison for life although, in his case, there was ample evidence of disturbance from an early age, as the jury heard at his trial and Tony Muggivan explained in an eloquent interview on Thursday's *News at One*.

He was five when he was taken to an assessment centre because he had told his mother about red worms coming out of his ears; soon after she died, he had begun going to sleep on her grave; he had started to take cars and guns when he was 12 or 13.

Mr Muggivan said O'Donnell was about 14 and on the run from Trinity House when he came to his home looking for food and a place to stay. He'd been living rough, in woods and sheds and old cars.

Mr Muggivan took him in for a while. So did others, but the gardaí were after him. And legal action seemed the only remedy.

As Mr Muggivan put it on radio: "I thought 'there's something wrong, a child couldn't be treated like this' and I took a case to have him released from Trinity House."

The action failed. O'Donnell was to spend many years, as a teenager and as a young adult, in custody in Ireland and in Britain. But Mr Muggivan is convinced he was not given the help he needed.

"I'm disgusted, really disgusted," he said on Thursday. "There was ample opportunity over the years to help him and it wasn't done."

True. Given the conditions in which O'Donnell lived and the fact that he and his family failed to receive serious attention, an outsider could be forgiven for imagining that this was a tale of a backward place in the 1950s.

But Brendan O'Donnell was born in 1974. What happened to him happened for the most part in the 1980s and 1990s. Most of the institutions through which he passed are still going strong.

As several local community leaders acknowledged this week, he had nothing going for him – and that included the services which, in theory at least, were meant to ensure that such failures didn't happen.

We are used to confronting old failures: allowing problem cases to fall between agencies, putting them to one side in the hope that they'll eventually take care of themselves by emigrating or dying.

We are all too familiar with local failures – of timidity or reluctance to interfere or an unwillingness to meet trouble halfway, the hope that someone else will do something.

Now, however, at the very moment of transition, when old certainties have been shaken and we need a set of values to replace those once imposed by a rigid, clerically dominated society, new voices are heard calling in harsher tones for a more callous order.

When Brendan O'Donnell terrorised his neighbours in Whitegate, the fear that spread to other parts of the country was conveyed with enthusiasm by some newspapers and some broadcasters for whom crime and fear had become an industry.

Reports of gangs roaming the countryside, robbing and attacking the old and vulnerable, filled the air. If it turned out that a crime was less dramatic than it first appeared, or of local significance only, too bad. The initial impression stood.

The result of O'Donnell's trial gave the crime industry a second opportunity to dramatise what he had done; his death was an unexpected bonus.

If Dr O'Connor sought support for his views, he would have found buckets of it in yesterday's editions of *The Mirror*, *The Sun* and *The Star*.

"May he rot in hell," screeched *The Mirror*. "Delight at triple murderer's death," *The Star* marked the "End of Sick Killer" – although as I understand it, the court found that O'Donnell wasn't sick. And *The Sun* reported the "Riddle of the Devil Killer's Death".

The souped-up reactions of these newspapers are at odds with the views expressed by some of those whose families were directly affected by O'Donnell's violence; but then it's not too difficult to find opinions that are more humane than the commentators who claim the common touch.

Father Joe Walsh's sister, Margaret Maher, told simply how she cried with relief when she heard the news of O'Donnell's death. (She called him Brendan.)

But there was no sense of vengeance in her comments on the events of May 1994. She remembered how Brendan looked in the court and how, if he were dressed in collar and tie, you might pass him in the street.

Presidency is an office which can be made to fit the holder

THE BUZZ OF speculation about the presidency tells us more about the concerns of parties and pressure groups than about would-be candidates and their ambitions for the office.

Support for the candidature of John Hume has suddenly grown this week: despite the silence of Mr Hume himself, there's been a scramble to promise him overwhelming endorsement. The rush may be premature, but to say so is apt to prove unpopular. It's as if to ask what his election might mean, especially to the people of Northern Ireland, is to question his suitability for the office.

But what are we to make of the promises of support from the main political parties? What do they tell us about the parties' confidence in their own would-be candidates?

What of their determination to learn from the experience of 1990 and the confidence which flowed then from a direct election? What of Labour's promise to make a campaign of it?

We have several weeks to wait before the parties announce their final choice of candidates and let us know whether they intend to play safe or to venture outside the political family.

One way or the other, there is time to let the electorate know what choice it has to make. The President may not be, in strictly legal terms, the Head of State; he or she is, as the Constitutional Review Group has it, the personification of the State. This doesn't mean that we must burden ourselves with someone who is pompous and remote when what we need is inspiration – a joyous and spirited advance into the new century.

Some say that an office holder grows into the office they're given.

The presidency, as Mrs Robinson has just proved, is an office that, with some limitations, can be made to fit the holder.

The Irish people have shown that they are also prepared to change, and to welcome change that seems in tune with the spirit of the time.

In Mrs Robinson's case, the proposal was put by Dick Spring and supported, in the first instance, by Proinsias de Rossa and others on the left. The movement broadened and deepened as it grew.

Mrs Robinson was endorsed, not by a clear majority of those who voted in 1990, but with a stronger combination of first and second preferences than either of the other candidates could muster.

Change had been proposed both before and after the election, not only by the political leaders who sought her candidature, but by Mrs Robinson herself and her close advisers.

Once in office, she was as good as her word. Not only did she convince us that change was desirable; from the moment of her election she set about showing how it could be done.

Not once, for the cameras; but again and again, whether the spotlight was on her or not.

And not just at home but in Northern Ireland, Britain and the rest of Europe, in the US and Africa.

It was not simply that she spoke, and spoke fluently in several languages, for the people of Ireland; she spoke to us about conditions endured by impoverished millions in a lopsided world and by those among us who are at risk of going unseen and unheard.

This was more than any other holder of the office had done; more than any of us had expected any holder of the office could or would do.

If people had been asked before she took her place in Áras an Uachtaráin whether Ireland was likely to choose as president a young and decidedly liberal woman, most would have said no. A few may have taken a braver view: "Maybe… but not in our time."

Now, here was someone unexpected – a young, articulate woman, at home in the modern world – doing unexpected things. Surprising not only those who'd been used to the old ways but many others who were equally limited by the new.

She drew attention to people who had so far gone unnoticed: not only those who needed help but those who worked to help their communities, with little recognition or public encouragement.

She worked on projects that were too arduous to be fashionable, like learning to speak Irish. She wasn't afraid of provoking controversy, as when she chose to shake hands with Gerry Adams.

She took risks, especially in the interests of the poor and hungry of central Africa, but made one of her few miscalculations at home when she decided to address the assembled TDs and senators in Leinster House.

Here she ignored the reality that advice to the other houses of the Oireachtas about issues on which they worked daily must sound redundant, if not patronising.

Overall, though, there were few complaints. Indeed, within a year of her arrival in office, we were beginning to wonder why we hadn't thought of this long ago.

As Mrs Robinson herself said, the presidency was a resource that hadn't been used. Now, the great majority of the electorate – including those who had voted against her – approved of the use to which she put it.

What had happened was that those who had proposed Mrs Robinson had taken the unusual step of first asking themselves what they wanted the presidency to be and the President to do. Then they set about finding someone who fitted the bill.

Mrs Robinson was that candidate. She recognised, and accepted, the limits which the Constitution imposed on the office. She also freed it from the constraints which political convention and the habits of 52 years had added to the constitutional limits.

She changed during her seven years in office. So did the presidency, though not as radically as, at times, her performance seemed to suggest. It is still far from an ideal home for a politician who savours the active life.

Now, two temptations have to be resisted.

One is to allow ourselves to slide again into the habit of generations and choose someone who is solemnly praised as statesmanlike but, in truth, is considered politically dispensable.

The other is to pretend that all we have to do is to follow willy-nilly the lead given in 1990 and attempt to recreate the current presidency by finding someone who, as nearly as possible, resembles Mrs Robinson.

These are temptations to be avoided. To return to the old ways would be to raise levels of cynicism that are already dangerously high – and seem likely to remain so until it's clear that such issues as political funding are being taken seriously. It would also ignore the lessons of 1990: the importance of asking what we want the presidency to be and the President to do in the next seven years.

The Constitutional Review Group, which reported more than a year ago, observed that the President, freed from executive functions – and the divisiveness which political activity would necessarily entail – serves as "a personification of the State".

"From the President," says the report, "the people seek a reflection of their highest values and aspirations."

DECEMBER 6th, 1997

Time for pendulum to swing back from smugness

THE FIRST 25 YEARS of the State ended without celebration. The 50th anniversary was overshadowed by the Arms Crisis and a sense of alarm at deepening divisions in the North.

Today, perhaps, we can begin to take stock of the 75 years of independence which began on December 6th, 1922.

And although this is a week in which Charlie McCreevy turned his back on a unique opportunity, shamefully deepening divisions he might well have reduced, we have much to celebrate.

At a glance the 75 years are easily divided and described: in the first 25, hardly anything changed; in the second, we all but died; but extraordinary advances in the last quarter-century have changed this society out of all recognition.

Such divisions are more easily suggested than sustained. One of the achievements of the early years was the Shannon Scheme, a triumph of engineering and imagination about which we might well have boasted in our new industrial age.

As for some of the social problems of the 1980s and 1990s – they take us back with a jolt to divisions we thought belonged to the 1950s. We are nothing if not contradictory, but then who isn't?

There's no denying that we were slow starters: if independence was the end of the centuries-old nightmare we'd been told about, we took our time waking up to reality and the new dawn.

We took our time and said little. In 1947, I was at school, aged 10, and an avid reader of what passed for popular history: Dorothy McArdle's wildly partisan fighting stories and tragedies of troubled times. At least they were livelier than the textbooks, all of which ended in 1916. But neither the fighting stories nor the official histories satisfactorily explained how we got from there to here.

In our corner of Clare, where so many had fought so hard for independence, no one celebrated its achievement 25 years on.

In many ways, we were still closer to the 17th, 18th or 19th centuries than to the 1920s.

On our shelves, the books our parents bought: Kickham's *Knocknagow*, which inspired de Valera's homely vision; Canon Sheehan's great novels, *The Blindness of Dr Gray* and *Glenanar*; Annie M P Smithson's stories of patriotic nurses: Butler's *Lives of the Saints* and the poems and prose of P H Pearse.

We paid much more attention to the 150th anniversary of the 1798 Rising (in 1948) than to the foundation of the State.

It was as if the Battle of Aughrim had happened shortly before the last fair of the 'Bridge. And we still felt the betrayal of Limerick, its treaty broken before the ink was dry.

Why did we hear so little about the beginnings of the State? Partly because it was a difficult birth and, as Roy Foster wrote, the Civil War "had created a caesura across Irish history separating parties, interests and even families and creating the rationale for political divisions that endure".

On one side of the caesura were those who'd presided at the birth, on the other the party that had governed without a break since 1932. It was easy to see why teachers who'd seen the two days might prefer the romance of James and William in the 17th century to the freshly laid minefields of the 20th.

Then there was the Catholic Church. Its control of health and education had long been secured in return for opposition to subversion in the 19th century.

Bishops condemned the Fenians and Parnell. But while some had doubts about the War of Independence, all eventually supported the establishment of the State.

Parish priests were managers of schools, chairmen of GAA clubs, leaders of community organisations and the moral policemen of their flock, in some cases with a degree of authority that a mullah of the deepest dye might envy. A teacher who dared cross them risked his or her livelihood – with additional penalties for challenging God's anointed.

If the pride of the parish or the glory of the little village were Kickham's (and Dev's) ideals, governments in the first 45 years of independence failed miserably to reach them.

This was no idyllic society for the landless or the urban poor. Servant boys slept on hay in many a farmer's loft, servant girls were paid 7s 6d (or 37.5p) a week.

In cities and towns, the lanes were populated by women their neighbours knew as shawlies and silent, staring children.

Authority was everywhere and it ruled by fear. It wasn't only policemen, teachers or priests who exerted control as a matter of course. Children were afraid of all adults and women often sacrificed – or were forced to sacrifice – health and happiness in the interests of husbands and families.

Secrecy was authority's fearful ally. There was a strong belief that, if you didn't talk about something, it didn't exist. In our small parish, where my father kept records for the parish priest, several cases of incest were noted. Noted but never publicly acknowledged – except by jeering children in the schoolyard or neighbours in the heat of an occasional feud.

Secrecy cloaked the removal of people from their homes, either because of an unwanted pregnancy or because they were being taken to the local mental hospital – signed in by relatives and, in many cases, never seen again.

There was so much to be ashamed of; so much that never came to light.

All of this was taken for granted. As was the pervasive affliction, tuberculosis, until the discovery of new forms of treatment and the arrival of Noël Browne in the inter-party Government of the late 1940s.

It took Browne to point to some other home truths – about the power of the Catholic Church and the selfishness of its allies in the medical profession: an alliance which still exists, though in a new form which has yet to be fully explored.

Browne's was the most striking of several brave advances which nudged the State towards the ideal Des O'Malley had in mind when he announced in 1985 that he stood by the Republic.

Fianna Fáil governments in the 1930s promoted vocational education, local industry and the interests of small farmers; Seán Lemass, as John Horgan recalls in his biography, won an argument with

Seán MacEntee and convinced his colleagues to follow Beveridge.

It took the reforming governments of Fine Gael and Labour (lately Fine Gael, Labour and Democratic Left) to lead the way towards more radical change. The left especially promoted openness and exposed the extent to which corruption has penetrated public life.

But standards of debate have fallen too, and in journalism as well as in politics. An American commentator lately complained, as others have done, about the absence of Catholic commentary in the media; nationalists consider themselves similarly excluded.

This is one of the legacies of a state which for 50 of the past 75 years, if not longer, timidly accepted conformity and what passed for tradition as the most secure and durable version of Irishness – Catholic, nationalist and immutable. It's a version of Irishness that has been challenged with some success. And the challenge must not be relaxed now that smugness has taken hold again.

DECEMBER 27th, 1997

When history repeats itself and no lessons are learned

LOUIS LENTIN'S *No More Blooms* was a great and shameful reminder of Ireland's dismal reaction to the Holocaust. The excuses were threadbare: we didn't know, we were poor and, in any event, we were neutral – as Éamon de Valera showed by signing the book of condolences on the death of Hitler. *Ar dheis Dé go raibh a anam.*

Eleven years later, when Church and State led popular reaction to the rising in Hungary and everyone knew what had happened, we were not so indifferent: an inter-party Government proposed to accept up to 1,000 refugees.

But within months of welcoming the few hundred who came, our attitude had changed to something sadly resembling the present cant: they had better be grateful, better still invisible; and, best of all, begone.

We may have been neutral during the Second World War but, when it came to the Cold War, no one could be under any illusion as to whom we were neutral against.

We'd prayed regularly for the conversion of godless Russia, sympathised with those we knew to be trapped behind the Iron Curtain and generally complained about anything, from film stars to ships, that had been tainted by communism.

The Archbishop of Dublin could forbid people to attend a soccer match against Yugoslavia and hope to be obeyed: those were the days when that was what bishops – and everyone else – expected.

(It was either a mark of Dublin's deep love of sport, or the first sign of wavering support for the bishops, when several people who'd been faithful to the GAA ban and had never seen as much as a kick of a foreign game turned up at Dalymount Park.)

The reason for the holy fuss was that, even as they kicked off in Dublin, Archbishop Stepinac was in one of Tito's jails in Belgrade. We found out later that he'd opposed the division of landlords' land, a scheme the Irish were bound to approve of. But bishops were bishops. And jail was jail. We'd seen what had happened to Oliver Plunkett, whose head was on display in a church in the town of Drogheda.

Hungary fitted our Cold War bill to a T. This was, as we thought, a Catholic country; small, struggling and under the heel of a powerful neighbour. Two leaders personified its spirit: Cardinal Josef Mindszenty and Imre Nagy.

Nagy was a reformer, who came to be highly regarded by some on the European left. He wanted to take Hungary out of the Warsaw Pact. What mattered to us, though, was that he was prepared to stand up to the Russians and for the cardinal.

At the beginning of November 1956, the tanks of the Soviet Union rumbled in and people, who'd armed themselves with rifles, shotguns and Molotov cocktails, took to the barricades. Mindszenty made a defiant speech and sought refuge in the American legation.

Ireland, which had been a member of the United Nations for less than a year, was one of 50 countries at an emergency session of the Security Council which voted for a United States-sponsored resolution condemning the invasion.

Our ambassador, Freddy Boland, explained why, in a speech neatly summarised by Joseph Morrison Skelly in *Irish Diplomacy at the United Nations 1945–1965*, published this year by Irish Academic Press:

> "[Boland] would return often to the concepts which imbued this speech: anti-communism; the national character of the Hungarian rebellion; Irish empathy for small nations callously invaded by powerful neighbours; the moral influence of the United Nations."

For this, and later efforts, Boland was excoriated by Father Dermot O'Doherty, described by Skelly as an unknown and unreasonable priest stationed in Minnesota.

His complaint had a familiar air of irritation: the ambassador was "pressing the rights of Hungary with more vigour than the rights of Ireland".

If the Irish delegation took no action to defend the minority in Northern Ireland, Father O'Doherty wrote, "suspicion will be confirmed that the present Irish Government (to which we might join the Irish bishops) is as zealous a defender of British interests as the British themselves. Woe to such a Government; woe to such a treason." Begob, it would put you in mind of the Fianna Fáil lads in Ennis during the presidential election. But Boland defended the Government, and the bishops. Ireland's line was checked with the Vatican and not found wanting.

The Minister for External Affairs, Liam Cosgrave, weighed in with comparisons between Ireland and Hungary. Hungarians were being deported to Siberia and he told the assembly that "mass deportation – or transportation as it was called in the dark phases of my own country's history – is one of the cruellest forms of political inhumanity".

The Minister might also have recalled that Arthur Griffith's interest in dual monarchy had been inspired by a Hungarian plan to reduce Austrian dominance in the Austro-Hungarian Empire.

In any event, Mr Cosgrave was doing no more than echoing popular sentiment. When the first groups – more than 160 – arrived at Shannon Airport on November 25th, 1956, thousands turned out to applaud them. The Mayor of Limerick, Ted Russell, and several priests were in the welcoming party.

Arthur Quinlan, who has reported on every event of any consequence in Limerick, Foynes and Shannon since the beginning of the war, remembers the eager reception and the transfer of the refugees to an army camp at Knockalisheen in east Clare.

But, as *The Irish Times* noted when they arrived, the Hungarians "had absolutely no desire to settle down to the listless and enervating life" to which refugees were condemned. They were already anxious to move on, to Canada if possible.

A spokesman for the group said: "We are labouring people and we would like to labour. They ask when and where we can go to labour." But in the 1950s, work was so scarce that 80,000 people were leaving the country every year.

The Hungarians were condemned to the listless life they'd hoped to avoid. Attempts to set up factories which might provide work ended in failure.

Arthur Quinlan also remembers how the mood changed as their frustration grew and in April 1957 many of the men and a few of the women among the 370 still in the camp went on hunger strike.

By early May, up to 20 who had collapsed were being treated in hospital and senior officials from the departments of external affairs and justice were called in to negotiate. Rumours of outlandish demands spread through Limerick. In fact, the refugees simply wanted to find a way out.

People who'd gathered sympathetically at the perimeter fence when they first arrived complained that they were as bad as the tinkers. When they got drunk and appeared in court they were lectured on ingratitude. This was Frank McCourt's city.

Comments in the Dáil, where Frank Aiken of Fianna Fáil had now replaced Mr Cosgrave, reflected changed attitudes. Bill Murphy of Fine Gael: "They have rashers and eggs for breakfast. Many of our own people have not. I would let them strike."

Donogh O'Malley (Fianna Fáil): "It should be made clear to the Hungarians what Ireland has done for them... They received no guarantee of employment here. If they don't like it, they are free to return."

Jack McQuillan (Independent): "Why were they brought here under false pretences?" Mr de Valera: "That isn't fair."

Is the only difference between the 1950s and the 1990s that some of us are better off?

APRIL 4th, 1998

Long and painful road to get to an agreement

TO BEGIN AT the beginning, there were strong words, two firm statements of intent: the Covenant of Ulster and the Proclamation of 1916. The Covenant was signed by 450,000 men in Belfast one day in September 1912. They pledged to stand by one another to defend "for ourselves and our children our cherished position of equal citizenship in the United Kingdom".

The Proclamation, read to the few bewildered onlookers who watched Pádraig Pearse, James Connolly and their troops march into the GPO that Easter Monday, was no less high-minded.

The signatories resolved "to pursue the happiness and prosperity of the whole nation and of all its parts, cherishing all of the children of the nation equally". But strong words, violence and the threat of violence were in the air. They chimed with the bloody and sacrificial spirit of the age.

The Covenant promised to use "all means which may be found necessary to defeat the present conspiracy to set up a Home Rule Parliament in Ireland". And, given that many of those who signed were members of the Ulster Volunteer Force, the threat was unmistakable.

Fear of a Home Rule conspiracy on one side, and Britain's divisive influence on the other, was to last a long time. The Proclamation declared the right of the Irish people to national freedom and sovereignty and its authors' determination to assert it "in arms in the face of the world".

Suspicions ran deep. If the unionists detected conspiracy, the nationalists declared themselves "oblivious of the differences [between majority and minority] carefully fostered by an alien Government".

Fear of a Home Rule conspiracy on one side, and Britain's divisive influence on the other, was to last a long time. It seeped through the political wastelands from the 1920s to the 1960s – until the frozen silence was broken by Seán Lemass and Terence O'Neill.

Indeed, it's still behind a barely hidden unionist conviction that its political opponents are too clever by half; behind some nationalists' belief that, whatever the unionists may say, the British Government holds the key to all doors.

On either side, whether fired by the Covenant or the Proclamation, only one feeling was stronger than suspicion and fear. It was the unshakable sense of being right.

Neither unionists nor nationalists needed formal declarations to tell them so: the truth was bred in their bones. They were gripped by a political and religious certainty, which some have compared to Stalinism.

Certainly those who'd been steeped in the rhetoric of 1916 were ready to accept the grand assumption in such phrases as "Ireland, through us", the claim by the leaders of the Rising to speak for all.

The first movement that most young people in the South knew and cheered in the 1940s and 1950s was the anti-partition campaign initiated by the inter-party Government that declared a Republic in 1949. And if some who took the rhetoric of anti-partitionism at face value set off on a different campaign in the 1950s that, too, was taken as a natural if over-enthusiastic response to the existence of the border.

It didn't occur to any of us who tramped through Limerick in Seán South's funeral in the mid-1950s that our view of the unionists – as Irishmen who'd been led astray – could be considered patronising, let alone proved wrong.

And when I went to work in Belfast, a few years later, I felt insulted by several unionist MPs serving in Stormont who had an equally patronising opinion of the Republic; they thought it a squalid and priest-ridden place.

It has taken North and South, unionism and nationalism, an unconscionable time to get to the point where clearer views of each other makes it possible to look forward to an agreement to share this small island.

Of course, it's more complicated than that. And we must all remember the hopes raised once before, when a settlement was attempted at the height of our shameful conflict, only to be shattered by a foolish gesture and the bullying force it unleashed.

The decision at Sunningdale to include a Council of Ireland in the agreement to set up a power-sharing executive – embracing politicians of all shades – gave the Ulster Workers' Council the excuse it wanted to bring the house down.

175

Others of both loyalist and nationalist persuasions still lurk in the shadows; groups claiming the inheritance of Covenant or Proclamation now bent on preventing even their erstwhile comrades from reaching agreement.

All they retain of the past, as they make, carry and set 1,000-lb bombs, is an attachment to violence – added to which there is now an indifference to the lives of the people they pretend to represent.

It's one of the reasons why the ritual dance of negotiation seems more frenetic than usual; it may even explain the contradictions between the private positions and public statements of some participants.

Some of those who've carried the heaviest workloads – tireless, patient people like Seamus Mallon, Reg Empey, Seamus Close, Monica McWilliams and David Ervine – seem most hopeful.

A few significant areas where resistance to agreement had been expected have produced mature and thoughtful responses to the prospect of change.

Rank and file members of Fianna Fáil were said to be holding tough on Articles 2 and 3. Most of those from Cork and Kerry who appeared on *Prime Time* during the week were reasonable and fair.

The most outlandish contribution was that of the editor of the *Sunday Business Post*, who came up with a vision of Bertie Ahern touring the country threatening immediate and terrible war if an agreement isn't accepted.

The most thoughtful long look at the negotiations, their historical and political contexts, is provided by Arthur Aughey of the School of History, Philosophy and Politics, University of Ulster, in the current edition of Democratic Left's theoretical magazine, *Times Change*.

He believes that what the Irish and British governments are seeking from the negotiations cannot be described as either unionism or nationalism. "The appropriate term," he writes, "would possibly be stabilism – the objective is to achieve stability and all else... is embellishment and detail."

The question to be solved, in Aughey's view, is:

"How can local politicians devise a rational and just compact amongst themselves and their communities in order to get out of a nasty and brutish state of nature and thus to secure conditions of peace, putting behind them the fanaticism of historic disputes?"

But "embellishment and detail" may prove highly significant as politicians struggle with symbolism and substance and the risk of failing to distinguish between them increases.

He ends with a quotation from the Duc de La Rochefoucald:

"Reconciliation with our enemies is nothing more than the desire to improve our position, war-weariness or fear of some unlucky turn of events."

MAY 30th, 1998

The old ghosts return to haunt Bertie

BERTIE AHERN PROVED in Belfast that he could live down the praise of his fatally flawed predecessor, Charles Haughey. Mr Ahern may well have been as devious and cunning as Mr Haughey believed; in the multi-party discussions on the future of Northern Ireland, he showed that he could be imaginative and courageous, too.

It took imagination, courage and tenacity to do what Mr Haughey and others in Fianna Fáil had long promised but, for fear of old ghosts and new ground, failed to achieve.

On arrival as leader, and again when he became Taoiseach, Mr Ahern made a point of reminding audiences that he'd promised another – perhaps more difficult – transformation.

This was a break with what had come to be considered custom and practice in some sections of the party, to the dismay and embarrassment of others who remembered commitments, not only to national unity, but to a fairer society in the Republic.

The custom and practice, which began with mohair-suited ministers and moneyed allies enjoying the high life in the 1960s, fell to earth with a thud last summer when Mr Haughey finally admitted that he'd lied, lied and lied again about his finances to the McCracken Tribunal.

The reappointment of Ray Burke seemed at odds with Mr Ahern's new-found high-mindedness. But the Taoiseach convinced many with his wide-eyed assurances that suspicions cast on his old friend had been thoroughly examined and satisfactorily allayed.

Mary Harney, too, seemed content, now that everyone had been given a clean bill of health by Mr Ahern – whose word she was pleased to accept – and by some of his most trusted lieutenants.

Dermot Ahern had been to London; the books at Fianna Fáil's offices in Mount Street had never been more thoroughly scrutinised; Mr Burke himself had been questioned by Mr Ahern and had assured his leader that everything was in order.

The only begrudgers, it seemed, were those who blamed the *Irish Independent*'s appropriately hard-nosed editorial favouring a Fianna Fáil–Progressive Democrats Coalition ("It's Payback Time") for their failure to retain office.

All of that was less than a year ago, and the sounds you now hear are of birds coming home to roost. The *Irish Independent* flaps its wings in distress and Ms Harney grits her teeth at having been kept in the dark until the last minute.

Mr Ahern is doing his best to recapture the breezy confidence of last year's election campaign, when he met more people and fewer questions than any politician since Alfie Byrne.

But he manages at every appearance to sound more like Mr Haughey or Albert Reynolds and, on occasion, even less convincing than either.

I'm speaking here of the Mr Haughey we knew – and never trusted – not the man who finally ran out of people to blame for his misfortune and acolytes to nurse his wounded pride.

It's the tone and style that's so familiar. No doubt there's a school where senior members of Fianna Fáil take lessons from some master of excuses and evasion, the Bart Simpson of politics.

Every hour on the hour, since the publication of *Magill*, the lines are repeated – by the Aherns, Bertie and Dermot, Michael Woods, Mary O'Rourke, Brian Cowen and, no doubt, others whom I haven't heard.

The lines are the Fianna Fáil version of Bart Simpson's "I didn't do it, nobody saw me do it, you can't prove a thing". They suggest some misunderstanding: "Oh, you mean that meeting. That payment. That cheque. That £30,000."

The trouble is this isn't a cartoon. There is no misunderstanding. And, given the rate at which John Bruton, Ruairí Quinn, Pat Rabbitte and Alan Shatter have been picking holes in it, it's no wonder the Government's case is in tatters.

The Taoiseach's announcement last night that all departments were to be put on Burke alert – reporting any decision in which the former Minister had been involved – is an attempt to stop the unravelling.

Until then, Mr Ahern and his colleagues had simply been insulting the intelligence of an electorate that has already shown its contempt for politics and politicians in the low turnout for the referendums.

Ministers made matters worse by claiming that Mr Ahern's

enquiries, conducted either before Mr Burke's appointment or at the time of his departure, were serious attempts to get at the truth of allegations, some of which had been in wide circulation for many years.

Dermot Ahern went to London to interview one man, and learned nothing he could rely on. He told Mr Quinn on *Prime Time* that he enquired no further.

The claim that Fianna Fáil should be credited with passing information to the Flood Tribunal (on planning) was even more ridiculous. As Mr Shatter pointed out, the tribunal went to the courts and won an order for discovery; to have disobeyed it would have been to invite action by the courts.

The Taoiseach said the first he heard of a £30,000 payment to Mr Burke by a Fitzwilton subsidiary, Rennicks, was in March. Then he admitted that Dick Spring might have told him about an anonymous letter on the issue last autumn. He wasn't sure.

But, even in March, it doesn't seem to have struck him that he might have done anything more urgent than wait for the Flood Tribunal to take its course.

And he waited until this week, on the eve of *Magill*'s publication, to tell the trusting Tánaiste what had been going on.

But, even by the standards of Fianna Fáil and Fitzwilton, the £30,000 paid to Mr Burke, in a cheque made out to 'cash' and handed to the Minister in his own home, was of high significance.

For this was no ordinary Minister and no everyday donor.

Mr Burke, as Mr Bruton pointedly told the Dáil, issued licences for the TV transmission system MMDS and, in the late 1980s, awarded 19 out of 29 licences to Princes Holdings, "a company associated with Independent Newspapers plc which is controlled by Dr Tony O'Reilly".

So the companies are part of a network which is richer than Goodman, more influential than Dunnes, with multiple interests and a powerful political weapon at its disposal, a group of newspapers with a dominant role in the Irish newspaper industry.

Fitzwilton insists that it contributes to political parties to support the democratic process; that the money paid to Mr Burke was intended for Fianna Fáil; and that the cheque was made out to cash because Mr Burke wanted it that way.

If these affairs are referred to the Flood or Moriarty tribunals, the method of payment, as well as the precise reasons for it, will no doubt be subject to more detailed examination.

Mr Justice McCracken wrote in his report on payments to politicians and to Mr Haughey in particular:

> "If politicians are to give an effective service to all their constituents, or to all the citizens of the State, they must not be under financial obligation to some constituents or some citizens only."

JULY 25th, 1998

Open door for fugitive funds, but closed shop for refugees

THE STORY OF de Valera and Peadar O'Donnell and the million who left keeps coming to mind. The old revolutionary, O'Donnell, and the founder of Fianna Fáil were mulling over the achievements of 30 years. Or so the story goes.

Some achievement, said Peadar. A million people have had to leave the country since you came to power, Dev.

Ah, but Peadar, said Dev, if you'd been in power it would have been no different. A million people would still have had to go.

Maybe so, said Peadar. Maybe so. But they'd have been a different million.

O'Donnell exaggerated. The crowd he wanted to be rid of could have travelled first class on the *Titanic*. Those who were forced out by unemployment and poverty-filled ships like the creaking *Princess Maud* on every tide.

The difference persists. It has grown and spread in the 30 years since Dev and Peadar had their chat. It's a striking feature of an immeasurably richer but increasingly unbalanced society.

You'll find evidence of division wherever you look: from the roaring inflation of the property market to the pole stuck through the roof of a house built for Travellers.

You'll find it in the OECD report which showed that 25 per cent of Irish people are at the lowest level of literacy, 50 per cent more than in other advanced countries surveyed.

And you'll find it, if you look beyond the occasional signs of surprise at our understanding attitude to genteel crime and political corruption, while judges banish the criminal poor to crowded jails in the manner of Victorian magistrates.

We've come a long way since the days of Dev and O'Donnell. The difference which once decided who'd have to leave now applies to those who must plead to be allowed in.

The authorities spend a hell of a lot more time preventing people from settling and working in this country than they spend preventing crooks from using it as a hiding place.

Tens of thousands of non-resident bank accounts are used to shuttle hundreds of millions in fugitive funds through the system. And Charlie McCreevy mutters vaguely about legitimate investors.

There are complaints about immigrants. And John O'Donoghue, who invented zero tolerance Irish-style, jumps to attention.

Extra staff in his department may help to speed the paperwork; for those who must wait, frustration is multiplied by a welfare system turned on its head, as if Kafka had a hand in it.

Immigrants draw welfare because they're not allowed to work.

And because they don't work, every bigot in the street feels free to call them spongers.

They're a burden on the State because the State doesn't allow them not to be. If they were playing with funny money or dodging the taxman, allowances would be made.

With luck, they might be given passports and introduced to someone who'd know where they could get top dollar on their investment.

So it was hardly surprising that reports which gleefully announced a drop in the levels of crime this week, passed on, without pause for thought, to the Haughey and Bula affairs.

It was as if what Charles Haughey is alleged to have done wasn't really a crime – certainly not in the same league as being accused of stealing a loaf of bread from a supermarket.

But that may be because reports on the business pages these days seem to be divided between warnings about inflation and investigations into financial institutions of one kind or another.

Once the spotlight was on Mr McCreevy's dirty dozen – welfare cuts which he felt obliged to introduce in the interests of the taxpayer, of course.

Now, it's Mary Harney's turn. Her dirty dozen are investigations into financial institutions and company affairs; and they're not the only enquiries going on.

Some complain that the lengthening series of tribunals – Hamilton, McCracken, Flood, Moriarty – is simply a way of getting judges to do the work of politicians while feeding the fat cats in the Law Library.

Others, who recognise the need for the investigations, wonder how we have come to this, gloomily suggest that we are somehow more prone to dishonesty than others and foresee a catastrophic end to the current affairs.

We are probably no less honest than others, though a tendency to cut corners has been developed – and even encouraged – over the years.

Our politicians are unhealthily close to people involved in finance, industry and commerce, and both politicians and business people share an addiction to secrecy.

Indeed, they manage to be both secretive and knowing, well-informed and suspicious; fearful of the public and anxious to resist every attempt to shed light on their affairs.

Not only are they anxious to avoid disclosure, they seem incapable of learning the lessons which involuntary disclosure provides.

They know that depending on business for funds is a dreadful way to run a party. But they won't change.

They have Mr Justice Brian McCracken's word for it that for a senior politician to find himself in a businessman's pocket is a short cut to corruption.

But when the Government published its proposals for the establishment of a permanent standards in public office commission, they turned out to be pathetic – whether cowardly or crooked, we will see when they come to be debated.

Politicians are often reluctant to apply what look like moral sanctions to each other lest they find themselves in the same predicament before the season is out.

But to allow oversight as an excuse for making a false declaration – among those who are supposed to be running the bloody show – is a mockery of the electorate.

The McCracken Report was a model of clarity. Someone has gone to great lengths to turn it into page after page of gobbledygook.

As for Bula and the activities of Jim Stanley: the free marketeers among us crowed at the collapse of the Soviet system and scorned any attempt to draw attention to what followed.

Now, they're complaining about the lack of regulation, the abundance of companies run by the Mafia and the absence of any serious attempt to come to grips with gangsterism.

In the case of Bula, with its much-hyped shares and expectations of sudden riches, it occurred to me that we'd heard something of this sort before, though without any suggestion whatsoever of any misbehaviour. The name Atlantic Resources comes to mind. As Matt Cooper wrote in *The Sunday Tribune* at the end of May: "Atlantic was one of the most hyped and ultimately under-performing stock market companies of the 1980s. But at one time it looked set to make [Tony] O'Reilly millions..." It didn't. He and others lost heavily on the venture. But neither the politicians nor the regulatory authorities appear to have learned anything from their misfortune.

NOVEMBER 7th, 1998

Republic of the rich and mean turns its back on world's poor

IT'S A SAVAGE irony that we should mark the 50th anniversary of the Universal Declaration of Human Rights with a miserly squabble about money.

Worse: it's a squabble about reducing the level of our aid to the poorest of the world's poor because our economy has been doing so well.

Liz O'Donnell, who has threatened to resign her ministerial post on the issue, used a threadbare cliché to describe it to the Dáil. She called it a problem of prosperity.

It's not. It's a problem of barely credible meanness and indifference; a shabby, shameful crux for a Republic which once prided itself as a leader among post-colonial nations.

We were in a poorer, but more honourable, state when we joined other developed countries in a commitment to the target set by the

United Nations for official aid to what was then known as the Third World.

That was in 1970. We had lately signed the Anglo-Irish Free Trade Area Agreement. We had yet to join the Common Market. If anyone had suggested that we might one day rank with the richest – and meanest – in the world, they'd have been trampled in the rush to see the blue moon.

The UN target was 0.7 per cent of the donor's gross national product. Not an outlandish demand, given the needs of the poor and the gap between poor and rich. We've never come within an ass's roar of that target.

For six years we've crawled towards the halfway mark. Last year we managed 0.31 per cent of GNP or £122 million. The Government's aim is to reach 0.45 per cent by 2002.

But, as Liz O'Donnell told Gay Mitchell, Dick Spring and Proinsias de Rossa in the Dáil, if the Estimate for aid remains unchanged, Ireland's contribution will be £137 million or 0.29 per cent in 1999 – not 0.32 per cent, as planned.

She'd written to the Minister for Finance and the Taoiseach, she told Sean O'Rourke on RTÉ Radio. "I have stated in plain language that our present level of aid is unsatisfactory," she told the Dáil.

On radio she said that she hadn't ruled out resigning on the issue; in the Dáil, Mr Spring encouraged her to convince her colleagues that the State should meet its international commitments.

If Liz O'Donnell resigns, she will be the first Minister since Frank Cluskey in the 1980s to have quit in support of a principle. Even if she doesn't, she will have drawn attention to yet another example of the triumph of hypocrisy over experience.

Few enough families in this country have escaped hunger, deprivation or exile. We should sympathise with people suffering the same fate who turn to us for help.

We should, but we don't.

Our laws insist that those who come here must not work. When they obey the law, we blame them for depending on welfare. Some say the money would be better spent on our own poor.

They don't mean it.

The ESRI suggested last week that we spend more on welfare. It was accused of "mindless prattle" by no less an authority than the chairman of the group set up to advise the Government on financial regulation.

There's a true tribune of the people and guardian of the public interest, comforter of the comfortable, the thinking man's Ivor Callely – Michael McDowell.

What the opponents of immigration really want is that anyone who feels tempted to come here should be encouraged to stay at home. If that doesn't work and immigrants arrive anyway, they should be sent back.

These are not the problems of prosperity. They are problems of bigotry and racism.

An outsider might have thought we were a generous people. And we are, proved so by the heroic work of thousands of volunteers, supported by funds to which tens of thousands contribute year in, year out.

To criticise this or other governments for failing to match such generosity is not to indulge in self-flagellation, as the hard chaws who snarl at the so-called poverty industry would have you believe.

The responsibility for official meanness and indifference in this instance lies not with the people, but with those who devised and passed the Estimates, those who chose to reduce or ignore the importance of overseas aid.

Some argue that we should look, not at the percentages, but at the cash value of the contributions.

But setting the target as a percentage of GNP in the first place made sense for obvious reasons: to take account of fluctuating fortunes in the donor states and to compare the performances of one donor state with another.

Defensive politicians and their media allies also urge the rest of us to keep things in perspective, to come down to earth and remember how life is in the real world.

In that case, they should be reminded that the £137 million currently set as Ireland's contribution to overseas aid falls far short of the cost of fraud in the beef industry.

Political cronyism and official connivance cost this State £70 million at one stroke and may cost us another £200 million before the dust settles on one of the sleaziest affairs in a period of unprecedented sleaze.

But the conniving politicians and officials of the late 1980s and early 1990s brazened it out. And their successors don't want to hear of it when the subject is raised by Des O'Malley or Pat Rabbitte.

No doubt they expect the law's delay and complex argument will fool the public into believing that the problems of prosperity being investigated by Mr Justice Moriarty, Mr Justice Flood and a dozen other adjudicators have gone away as well.

In the meantime, the Government is engaged in another remarkable exercise, campaigning for a seat on the Security Council of the United Nations.

It's remarkable because anyone engaged in such a campaign might be expected to ensure that its own house was in order, its record sound, its standing in the international community at least as respectable as its peers and potential competitors.

There's no doubt about our solid contribution to peacekeeping. But can we any longer claim to bridge the gap between developed and developing countries?

Can a country which has the highest current and predicted growth levels in the European Union but the poorest record in overseas aid look other UN members in the eye as it canvasses support?

In some broadcast discussions among commentators, the issue has been reduced to a minor theme in a wider debate about Mary Harney's leadership or the future of the Progressive Democrats.

I think it's about two things: our role in an impoverished world and national self-respect.

DECEMBER 12th, 1998

New party of the left must insist on primacy of politics

THE ASSUMPTION IS often made that you can have equity or efficiency, a fair society or a profitable economy – but not the two together.

One of the biggest challenges facing Labour and Democratic Left as they join forces today is to prove that this is not so. Equity and efficiency are not mutually exclusive.

This has to be at the core of the left's approach at a time of extraordinary prosperity, deepening division and increasing uncertainty about the direction of Irish life.

First, however, it means showing that, in spite of the abuses of some politicians and the woeful inefficiency of others, politics is not a dirty word.

Equity and efficiency never were mutually exclusive, although they've long been confused with patronage, whether those patronised were businesslike cronies at one end of the scale or impoverished clients at the other.

The political roots of this confusion were in the two-party system, where it was easy to see who was who: the fellows with the caps were the Labour crowd. The men they saluted belonged to Fianna Fáil and Fine Gael.

Labour knew its place and its obligation to wait (in the national interest). Fine Gael would share power with it when the time was right, in Fine Gael-led coalitions.

Fianna Fáil would look after its constituents as assiduously as if they were its own: it was a classless society and this was the natural order of things.

Now, there are other myths just as clearly designed to throw the public off the scent of power, privilege, influence and corruption. The message sounds different. The line of argument is the same.

It used to be said that Labour could safely leave the serious stuff to Fianna Fáil and Fine Gael. Now, the claim is that nothing can be changed, certainly not by politics, definitely not by the left.

Two criticisms are heard again and again. One is that all parties have moved to the centre – so there's no real difference between them. No conflict. No contest of ideas. No choice for the electorate. No alternative government.

The other is that all the real decisions are made either by the European Union or by big business, as often as not in secret, with a minimum of discussion and little or no reference to the electorate.

The European Union is a political as well as an economic entity. All but two of its members are governed by left-wing or left-led administrations. The most powerful group in the parliament are Social Democrats.

The EU leaders now gathered in Vienna are meeting under the presidency of a new German Government of Social Democrats and Greens. The issues under discussion in the EU – the Budget, structural funds, regionalisation and, in due course, the harmonisation of taxes – are of particular significance in Ireland.

We are no longer a poor state dependent on richer neighbours. It's becoming clearer by the week that a new approach to EU affairs is essential; so are new allies and a keener sense of what's happening in the wider world.

Already, there is the beginning of a debate about contrasting ways of tackling social and economic affairs that sets the European approach against the American.

It's a debate that will determine the direction of this society in the next 10 to 20 years, and it's showing up serious ideological differences.

On one side are those who favour the market alone as an arbiter of how our needs are met, essentially how our society is to be organised. Call it the Ryanair way. On the other are those who believe the public interest is best served by partnership and regulation, by what their opponents gleefully deride as the nanny state.

The debate isn't confined to the political arena. Indeed, few politicians have chosen to identify themselves with the American way, and some in the catch-all parties are distinctly uneasy about taking sides. Some complain that the left assumes it has a monopoly of morality, as if morality was a section of the political market to be cornered by the first comer.

The truth is that, on the increasingly important issue of standards in public life, the left is best placed to lead the way. At present, by all accounts, it's strapped for cash.

Paradoxically, that gives it an advantage over parties that have deeper pockets but real or presumed obligations to their sponsors.

Besides, the left has a much more impressive record than its opponents or their camp followers in the media.

Labour and Democratic Left, with such honourable members of other parties as Des O'Malley, have consistently demanded openness and accountability.

Labour promoted the laws on freedom of information and ethics in office, for which Eithne Fitzgerald was roundly criticised by the conservatives of Fianna Fáil and Fine Gael before winning their grudging support. Her efforts were derided by some commentators and ignored or misunderstood by others, for whom politics is a dirty word.

The left demands the protection and promotion of the public

interest; the right complains about what its industrial and media allies call the nanny state. The left insists on openness and accountability; the right argues that in the real world – a place the unemployed, the poorly paid and the handicapped clearly know nothing about – life doesn't work like that.

There is a suggestion that not only are equity and efficiency mutually exclusive, the efficient by the very nature of their enterprise are special cases – and entitled to cut corners.

But cutting corners, as we've seen, leads to some riding roughshod over the planning laws, company laws, financial regulations and other controls designed to ensure that in this Republic every citizen is bound by the same code.

The left more consistently than any other group hammers home a message of political responsibility: when ministers refuse to answer questions in the Dáil or politicians appear to use their positions for personal gain, they must be held to account.

The left is not alone in its insistence, but it is the most consistent. It has made political mistakes and paid for them. It has shed most if not all of its foolish rhetoric.

The most telling events of the week, however, were the revelations by Mr Justice Flood and Mr Justice Moriarty of failures to co-operate with tribunals established by the Oireachtas to investigate issues implicating politics and business.

The new party can do no better than insist on the primacy of politics.

The damage Haughey and friends did lives after them

WHEN DES O'MALLEY said on Wednesday that this democracy may be "in more trouble than any of us realise", he wasn't just making a point for argument's sake.

He was expressing an unease that has spread and become deeper during the past year as the State reluctantly comes to recognise the extent and depth of corruption that has overshadowed public life.

Of course, Mr O'Malley was speaking for the Progressive Democrats, specifically of their belief that those in high office should abide by "normal and reasonable standards of honesty and decency in dealing with affairs of state".

"If we are to be criticised for holding that position," he said, "then this democracy is in more trouble than any of us realise."

But it wasn't simply a partisan position, nor was the threat implicit in the speech confined to the fate of the irreparably damaged Fianna Fáil–Progressive Democrat Coalition. That threat was there, large as life. But there was a bigger challenge to parties and to politics:

"All of us in this house can help to restore public confidence in the Irish political system, or we can abandon our responsibility…"

And if that happened:

"There is a political movement out there now, watching current developments very closely. That movement has recently put itself forward as the real anti-sleaze party in Irish politics. I refer to the so-called Republican movement, the people who murdered Jerry McCabe."

Mr O'Malley's credibility has been earned over decades of unselfish service. It's helped by clear thinking and an ability to express concerns that often lurk below the surface of public life.

The public has understandable difficulty in coming to terms with the state of affairs uncovered by the series of tribunals that began, inauspiciously, with Hamilton and shows no sign of running out of issues to investigate.

What worries people is not just the scale of events, the huge sums carelessly changing hands, the cunning schemes, the absent-minded arrogance, the apparent indifference to anything that couldn't be counted as power, influence and profit; it's the mind-boggling meaning of it all.

And yes, they must conclude, we have had at the head of affairs in this State one of the most devious, ruthless and selfish politicians we've known. In politics and business, he kept (and was kept by) a circle of friends who knew that once they played the game, everything was up for grabs.

Some once fondly imagined that Charles Haughey was a bit of a rogue, liable to be feathering his own nest. So what if he was, they said, he was also roguish on our behalf – for the good of the oul' country.

It was a comforting thought in a way – the reason why John Healy, who once occupied these columns, referred to Honest Jack (Lynch) and Garret the Good (FitzGerald) and managed to make them sound like an insult to both.

The contrast was with Charlie the Chancer; the implication was that he was neither honest nor good, the assumption that, maybe, we were all the better for that.

Those who argued that we were not were dismissed as cranks, soreheads, not real men. Real men were sound on the national question and capable of running the State; they were at home with hard-nosed businessmen, at ease in the company of their peers.

Natural leaders like Mr Haughey were full-blooded men who had no time for shilly-shallying, backsliding or disloyalty in the party, not to mention carping from the opposition.

He needed to show a strong hand here if he was to hold his own in international company with fellow statesmen, Helmut Schmidt of Germany and Valéry Giscard d'Estaing of France, or fellow guests in the George V in Paris.

But there was no public interest or, if there was, it came a poor second to the personal or corporate interests of his circle of friends. The fellow patriots who came to the aid of Celtic Helicopters, as you may read in Mark Brennock's report today, didn't have to wait too long for their rewards.

The currency was familiar: private investment for the benefit of the family firm in exchange for substantial benefit at the expense of the State.

Those who, even now, excuse the leader who stamped his inimitable style on the party, the Government and the State still say that all of this could not have been achieved by one man. It wasn't. That's why the tribunals were set up. It's also why some old Haugheyites wait nervously for the call. And it's why the challenge to repair the damage done to public life extends not only to Bertie Ahern and Fianna Fáil but to their coalition partners and the parties in opposition.

This, as well as the Government's tenuous grip on affairs, is what adds to the importance of the weekend's Fine Gael ardfheis. The party starts with a ready-made advantage: the fact that, in spite of some similarities, and the questions that hang over one erstwhile Minister and probably some councillors, it's not Fianna Fáil.

But it must find more to say for itself than that. Mr O'Malley expects that standards will be an issue in the general election. He's right.

The election will also be about the increasing divisions in our society, the poor state of public services, the crisis affecting small farmers – essentially about the redistribution of resources.

John Bruton was at his best as Taoiseach and, paradoxically, most persuasive, when he struck a social-democratic note in the final debate of the 1997 campaign.

The people of this State have had the present coalition's payback time: longer waits for hospital treatment; house prices, as an auctioneer observed this week, beyond the means of teachers and nurses; garda cars on the streets chasing welfare fraudsters.

The jails are full of people who've never had a chance in life. The real chancers are to be found elsewhere.

Fianna Fáil doesn't look as if it's up to the challenge it faces. Any party that sends Brian Cowen out to bat for it on an issue of public confidence and some sensitivity can't be thinking straight.

Mr Cowen's bluster and arrogance simply remind the public what a bloody awful job he's doing in the Department of Health.

Nor does the buck stop with politics. It's easy to sneer at politicians these days, equally easy and false to claim that "they're all the same".

Business is at least as seriously in need of reform. So are the media. And accountants claim to be able to regulate their own affairs – as if they belonged to some genteel club that never helped a fraudster across a line.

Des O'Malley put it up to colleagues of all parties in the Dáil: either they could face up to the challenge to politics or they could resort to "cute hoorism".

The rest of us should recognise that, for cute hoors to survive, they need the support and connivance of a hell of a lot of village idiots.

All guns in Fianna Fáil armoury trained on the media messenger

MICHEÁL MARTIN WORE his most plaintive face for the six o'clock news: "People," he said, were "sick and tired of the allegations that are coming out."

He's right, of course; except that he and his colleagues are beginning to blame the opposition, *The Irish Times* and anyone but Fianna Fáil for the political oil slick now drifting in on every tide.

What worried Mr Martin was Geraldine Kennedy's latest instalment in the familiar series, 'Passports for Sale'.

He wasn't the only senior member of the party to be alarmed by the report. Bertie Ahern, Mary O'Rourke and Jim McDaid were, in turn, dismissive, angry and indignant.

They'd been on edge before its publication. All week they'd been watching the news from the Moriarty Tribunal, where the lordly life and extravagant times of Mr Ahern's mentor, Charles Haughey, were being exposed in fascinating detail.

Here was a Fianna Fáil leader and Taoiseach whose political ambition had been matched by an appetite for conspicuous consumption and a stunning indifference to who paid for it.

The last thing his erstwhile colleagues wanted was to have the public reminded of his modest successor's political provenance. Government and its allies in the media did what they could to kill the story.

It didn't work.

The passports-for-sale scheme, which allowed wealthy investors to become citizens, was introduced by Mr Haughey in the late 1980s. (It, too, has now been discredited and abandoned.)

In the early 1990s, the passport seeker in question was asked by an Irish businessman-turned-passport-broker to contribute to Fianna Fáil. A bank account was opened for the purpose.

The money in the account was transferred to a Fianna Fáil account in the names of Albert Reynolds, as leader, and Bertie Ahern, as treasurer.

On Thursday morning, Mr Ahern called *The Irish Times* report "a load of lies" and "a ball of smoke". His tone was aggressive. The groupies were impressed. In the Dáil on Thursday afternoon, he quibbled with definitions.

Had the money been transferred or diverted? Was the original account an investment account or an investor's? Was the money a contribution to Fianna Fáil or a loan (interest-free and not yet repaid, eight years later)?

As he pointed out, there was nothing illegal about the payment of £10,500 to Fianna Fáil.

But it had the whiff of transactions in countries where the practice of dashing – to sweeten local officials and politicians – is taken for granted by visiting businessmen.

A friend of mine who directed engineering projects in the Middle East and Nigeria once explained that dashing was part of the job – the way they do things there, he said.

The way we do things here – and, more to the point, the changes that ought to be made in electoral practices, party funding and ethics in public life – is only beginning to be discussed.

But the discussion will get nowhere if the reaction to those who raise questions is, as it was this week, one of suspicion that partisan or unspecified interests are being served.

Not-so-humble backbenchers like Mary Hanafin seemed convinced that the party's critics, egged on by persons unknown, were up to their necks in a plot to destroy the Government.

It was as if opposition was, by definition, subversive and

questioning was inherently dangerous. (Plots are unnecessary when a government is bent on self-destruction.)

Fianna Fáil is indeed being criticised by the opposition and by some writers and broadcasters with varying degrees of consistency and enthusiasm.

It would be mighty odd, given the news from Dublin Castle, if questions were not asked about events that gave rise to two tribunals, a dozen other inquiries and numerous disclosures in the media.

And, since most – though not all – of the politicians under investigation were leading members of Fianna Fáil, it follows that most of the questions are about the party's handling of its own and the State's affairs.

The most serious threat to the Government comes from within. It's raised by the conduct of senior members of Fianna Fáil, past and present, and the worry that the patience of the Progressive Democrats may snap at any time.

Younger deputies find it hard to take. They emerged from the Dáil this week repeating Mr Ahern's claim that his was a clean Government, cleanly led, and hoping for an end to complaints and criticism.

But Mr Ahern's performance in the Dáil bore too many reminders of past performances for comfort – beginning with outright denials, ending in prevarication and confusion.

The young deputies should be reminded that much of the information that has been confirmed by tribunals first saw the light, perhaps in a different form, in reports which were denied, dismissed or became the subject of libel threats when they first appeared.

Charlie McCreevy took a more cynical view of the media. He suggested on Monday that Bertie Ahern's trouble was that he was too accessible to journalists – too willing to answer questions.

And later, Mr McCreevy spent the best part of an hour discussing his own career and opinions on RTÉ Radio with Vincent Browne.

Someone on Mr Ahern's staff had anticipated the problem during the 1997 election campaign. The party leader swept from end to end of the State on a wave of goodwill. He shook thousands of hands, hugged hundreds of admirers, smiled and was gone.

He didn't answer questions. At most stops, he wasn't asked any. Those who covered the campaign wrote about the handshakes, the smiles and the speed. 'People Before Politics' was the slogan; politics was a dirty word.

He lost the only serious debate he took part in, but by then it didn't matter. He had the weight of Tony O'Reilly behind him and a mind-numbing fog of show business all around.

The Independent Group joined in the defence of Mr Ahern yesterday, with a call for responsibility and the need to avoid the damaging effect of repeated allegations.

There was no mention of the *Irish Independent*'s decision to publish Geraldine Kennedy's report on Thursday.

It's good to know that in Middle Abbey Street we have competitors who are not too blind to recognise a good story – and not too proud to lift it.

MARCH 6th, 1999

Ahern has not eluded smothering influence of the past

IF THERE ARE plans to revive *The Odd Couple*, let me be the first to put in a word for Bertie Ahern and Pádraig Flynn. Jack Lemmon and Walter Matthau were made for the parts; at their meeting in Brussels on Wednesday, Bertie and Pádraig showed they were natural stand-ins.

Even before he lumbered into shot, the Commissioner could be heard sonorously reminding the members of his Cabinet, "I believe we have some guests."

The camera and the Commissioner found the visitor together. He stood, uneasily, alone in the Irish Ambassador's residence, waiting to be discovered: "Ah, Taoiseach Bertie," the Commissioner boomed. "How are you?"

As they and the camera circled each other, Taoiseach Bertie muttered that he was in great form. The Commissioner ignored the tone. "Good-to-see-you," he boomed. "Good to see you indeed." It didn't look like it. They touched hands.

Taoiseach Bertie pawed the ground and eyed far corners of the room. Only when the Commissioner introduced his Cabinet did Taoiseach Bertie smile.

Tommie Gorman sounded like someone who had come to measure the body language. Or, like Cilla Black on *Blind Date*, wishing the lucky couple well. Not since Tommie had shouted questions on one side of a closing door and the Commissioner had stood mute on the other had he enjoyed such a moment.

The interviewer drew another blank. The Commissioner said there was no need to go into detail about what had been said. The matter was now settled until it came up at the tribunal.

Taoiseach Bertie pawed the ground again and said there had been no discussion, "…other than Pádraig Flynn and myself going through the door together. I thanked him for sending me the letter because I was looking for it for some time."

The letter didn't mention the £50,000 that Tom Gilmartin claimed to have given Mr Flynn, but it did say Mr Flynn had been requested by the tribunal not to discuss or divulge any matters discussed with the tribunal.

But, Fine Gael and Labour had asked, how could this be squared with Mr Flynn's *Late Late Show* appearance?

Taoiseach Bertie and the Commissioner had met dozens of times since Tom Gilmartin made his claim but, with the delicacy for which they're both well known, they avoided the subject.

Another curiosity: their last meeting had been on December 23rd, though by general consent the most critical EU negotiations for decades are under way and Taoiseach Bertie says the Commissioner's role is pivotal.

Indeed, one of the reasons given for avoiding any serious discussion of the (missing?) £50,000 has been the need to keep relations between Dublin and the Commissioner on an even keel.

Now, it seems that two key figures in the negotiation – Taoiseach Bertie and the Commissioner – barely talk to each other.

Then, you remember, these are no ordinary relationships, and the party is no ordinary party. This is the leader who, as treasurer, was joint holder of a party account but didn't notice a donation of £10,500 arrive in it.

This is the Taoiseach who, when told of the £50,000 that apparently hadn't found its way to the party, said: "Don't tell me, tell the tribunal."

This is the leader who, on the point of placing Ray Burke in his Cabinet, could only find it in his heart to ask if there was anything worrying him.

The leader who climbed every tree in north Dublin and came down empty-handed; who packed Dermot Ahern off to London with a single question that he brought home unanswered.

This is the politician who answered one of Mr Gilmartin's claims by reference to the Taoiseach's diary, except that the diary was in Charles Haughey's custody and someone considered friendly to Haughey had to be sent to Kinsealy to check it.

Mr Haughey himself stood charged with obstructing the McCracken Tribunal, yet Mr Ahern took his word for the contents of the diary and trotted it out in the Dáil as if it were irrefutable.

Mr Ahern is regularly acknowledged by politicians and commentators as someone who has escaped the smothering influence of the past.

Given the examples cited here and his reluctance to meet challenges like the Flynn case, it doesn't look like it.

Of course, Mr Ahern and his pompous colleague in Brussels aren't the only leaders of public opinion who've presented us with examples of diplomatic deafness and indifference this week.

Liam St John Devlin explained to the Moriarty Tribunal on Thursday why the question of Mr Haughey's debt was never on the AIB board's agenda.

> "The reason," he said, "is that there was a general feeling among the board of directors that the less they knew about him the better...

> "One could infer from the general mood of the directors that it was better not to know too much because of the extreme sensitivity of the matter based on Mr Haughey's standing and the extent of national support for him."

A retired chief executive of AIB, James Fitzpatrick, put it more succinctly:

> "If he had a very strong following and if we took action that was seen to be damaging to him, it could have repercussions on the bank's business."

And this is the bank, the national institution, which saw fit to dismiss in crude and deceptive terms a report by Des Crowley of the *Evening Press* which came closer than any other to the truth of Haughey's financial standing in the early 1980s.

Haughey was not, as many of his admirers thought (and think), some latter-day Robin Hood. He may have been out to rob the rich – AIB and the people from whom his agents begged or borrowed money. The funds didn't go to the poor; he served himself. Indeed, the public policies he followed in the late 1980s were crudely based on those of the Prime Minister he hated most, Margaret Thatcher.

The cuts in public services, which he first opposed, then implemented, had the backing of two outfits he despised – Fine Gael and the banks – and the support of many commentators.

But he was never much bothered by the source of support; he thrived on the acquiescence of those, in AIB or politics, who didn't care to ask too many questions for fear of what they would find out.

MARCH 20th, 1999

Why the press and pundits gloated at Oskar's fall

OSKAR LAFONTAINE'S RESIGNATION as Germany's Finance Minister is greeted with ill-concealed relief by the Irish Government and gloating by many commentators.

But what has Mr Lafontaine done to worry the Government? And what was he planning to do that representatives of the new right found so threatening?

The European Commission is forced to resign. But what were the commissioners accused of?

And how will the changes that are bound to follow affect us? Apart, that is, from the Government's exquisite dilemma about what to do with Pádraig Flynn.

The callous murder of Rosemary Nelson is rightly linked to that of her fellow lawyer Pat Finucane. But is it not also linked to the bombing of Omagh?

Both Ms Nelson's murder and the Omagh bomb were intended to provoke violent reactions which would, in turn, inflame smouldering resentment and threaten the Belfast Agreement.

The public sessions of the Moriarty and Flood tribunals have come to a halt for the time being, allowing commentators to take stock and issue their own interim reports.

But it seems that, in some cases at least, writers and broadcasters have missed or forgotten the point. The tribunals were set up to investigate payments to politicians and what amounts to a shadowy connection between business and politics.

How the payments first came to light is – like a variety of other sideshows – a titillating diversion. It may be popular and, indeed, profitable; it may also be what some of those with most to lose would like the rest of us to see as the main event.

Powerful and persistent forces are out there, working as hard and as cleverly as the law allows (there's no shortage of resources) to prevent us keeping our eyes on the ball.

Keeping our eyes on the ball, on the central importance of politics and on the interests of the Irish people as a whole, is what this piece is about.

That astute judge of international affairs, Charlie McCreevy, who took an airily dismissive view of the economic crisis in the Far East, had described Oskar Lafontaine as a socialist of the old school.

When Lafontaine resigned, some of McCreevy's media allies took up where Dinjo left off and danced jigs on the radio – mostly on Today FM.

With raucous delight and the zest the London tabloids usually display when dealing with football oddities and freakish foreigners, they chortled on about Mad Oskar and conjured images of their own hero doing cartwheels in Merrion Street.

But what Lafontaine had been trying to do was what might have been expected of any serious Social Democrat.

He wanted to spread the burden of taxation, to stimulate demand and employment and, by changing the laws on citizenship, among other reforms, to make Germany a fairer and more welcoming society.

German industry feared increasing corporate taxes and the

popular German press, as usual, supported the approach adopted by its proprietors and their industrial allies.

It shouldn't surprise that, in this country, conservative politicians and commentators find they have more in common with German industry and British tabloids than with the German people.

And when it comes to tax harmonisation or related reforms, as proposed by the German Social Democrats, the Coalition and its noisy cheerleaders will be found, not tumbling in the street, but with their backs to the wall.

Fear of foreigners, especially those with funny guttural accents, has always played a part in British resistance to the European Union.

And when the commission was forced to quit on the strength of a report alleging, we were led to believe, all manner of malpractices, it was open season on the EU's most notorious high-flyers.

Hot on the heels of Red Oskar came Mad Jacques, Evil Edith, a clutch of Italians, Greeks, Spanish and Portuguese – with their extended families – and, enigmatic as ever, Puffed-Up Pádraig from Castlebar, telling us it's for Taoiseach Bertie and himself to decide where he stands.

But, as Pádraig swanned past would-be interviewers, like a galleon in full sail, it must have occurred to Irish television viewers that the case against the commission was not what we'd been led to believe. A little lacking in meaty detail.

Commissioners didn't know what was happening in their services. There were a few cases of nepotism or cronyism (someone's brother-in-law got a job, someone else's dentist).

The trouble began, as a rule, once projects were farmed out to private enterprise. As John Palmer reported here, more than 80 per cent of all fraud affecting EU spending occurred under the responsibility of national governments, not the commission.

Now, that's more like it, as we know only too well. We've had the tribunal and paid the price. The commission's offences are small beer by comparison, the kind of stuff that has to be worked on before it's built into headlines suggesting damning indictments and the like.

The real challenge is to increase the commission's accountability, which means adding to the parliament's powers and opening up the relationships of parliament and commission with the ministerial councils and heads of government.

The commission, which functions as a secret society, also has other defects that need to be removed. It has too much to do and too few people to do it.

But Ireland has always been opposed to change that would enhance the democratic force of institutions deemed favourable in their present forms to the interests of small nations.

It's time we examined the case again, this time in the context of rising demands for accountability and what may turn out to be profound institutional change and development.

Change and development on all fronts was challenged by the murder of Rosemary Nelson. It showed how desperate some forces have grown in their efforts to prevent movement in the direction of the Belfast Agreement.

For this was not just a sectarian killing; those who planned it aimed at the most dangerous point in a vulnerable community's nervous system. If they'd succeeded, the agreement would have been paralysed.

A wounded but determined people resisted the Omagh bombers, the so-called Real IRA; given the leadership they are promised once more, the same people will resist the so-called Red Hand Defenders. They have the same intent.

Of course, there are commentators and activists who would prefer if we took our eyes off the ball and reduced the ideals of the Belfast Agreement to the ashes of mutual destruction.

At a different level, interested parties of another hue are anxiously attempting to persuade us that what will matter when business resumes at Dublin Castle is how someone sounds in the witness box – not how we succeed at cleaning up a national mess.

A shameful silence as the children suffered

"Exactly 30 years ago, a commission of inquiry into industrial and reformatory schools made a report to the Government. It was full of recommendations for reform.

"Some of them were adopted but many others, even more essential to the welfare of the children, were neglected."

THE WRITER WAS Michael Viney. His series, 'The Young Offenders', appeared in this newspaper exactly 33 years ago; the piece from which the extract is taken was published on May 4th, 1966.

The commission to which he referred had published its findings in 1936. The first part of Mary Raftery's heartbreaking series *States of Fear* was broadcast on RTÉ 1 on Tuesday.

Michael Viney listed the charges against Irish society for which he offered evidence. The first was "that most juvenile offences in the Republic are rooted in social conditions: urban poverty and overcrowding, deprivation and inadequate family welfare".

States of Fear is not about offenders, but, as the lives of orphanages, industrial schools and reformatories are exposed, the sense that this was in essence a penal system is unavoidable.

And as we look again at these and other issues – the administration of justice, the operations of banks, the links between business and politics – it's plain that the most pervasive influence on Irish society is class.

Class governs access to health services, housing and education; the work we do, the environment we live in, the air we breathe. It makes most difference to those who are at the remote and all but invisible end of what can scarcely be called a scale.

Why this has not given rise to class politics, as in other industrialised societies, is a subject fit for the Labour Party, whose delegates have gathered this May Day in Tralee.

For Labour, class is of more – much more – than academic interest. The shape of our society is changing, as the middle ground expands and those above or below it – the top 10 and the 25 per cent at the bottom – lose touch with the mainstream.

The nature, if not the shape, of society remains as it was.

Class and the imperative to maintain control linked Maynooth and Dublin Castle long before independence; with the fusion of Church and State in the 1920s, the system of social and economic division looked like becoming permanent.

States of Fear has set people asking why no one lifted a finger on behalf of the children left to the mercy of our industrial schools and orphanages in the 1940s, 1950s and for much of the 1960s.

Some blame the Catholic Church. A clerical threat certainly hung over the heads of teachers, much as the threat of Daingean or Glin was used to subdue their pupils.

The press wouldn't say boo to a goose. The *Irish Independent*, a respected and authoritative newspaper, was too busy with Lenten pastorals. The *Irish Press* sheltered a fine collection of sacked schoolteachers, spoiled priests and lapsed republicans but, with Fianna Fáil in power, steered clear of controversy.

So did Radio Éireann and the *Cork Examiner*, as they then were; and *The Irish Times*, selling fewer than 30,000 copies a day, hardly mattered.

Could it be that no one knew what was happening? It's hardly credible; far more likely that because the poor, the excluded, the people who didn't fit in, were considered a threat to society, they were best left alone.

When Michael Viney's series appeared, revelation was followed by shock but, only at a safe distance, by change.

We were told then, as we are being told now, that the religious orders were doing what the State couldn't or wouldn't do; that we – and the children they looked after – ought to be grateful to them.

Mary Raftery has come up with a radically different view: the State was paying all along; the religious orders were making a profit from the meanness inflicted on the children.

The State was paying the piper but the politicians, civil servants and the rest of us were too timid, too ignorant or too content to insist that it was our right – and responsibility – to call the tune.

Could the Department of Education not have known what was going on in schools that were partly or wholly under their control? I doubt it. And so does *Magill* in its April issue.

But whenever there's a fuss we hear the same professional defence: the system works. The fact that there's a fuss is proof of it. Wrong on both counts: systems of self-regulation by and large don't work.

The claims that they do are usually made after something untoward has been discovered – by accident. And the accompanying claim is that it's all over now, nothing of the kind will ever happen again.

The answer to such po-faced assurances is: how can they tell? Since whatever has been discovered came as a complete surprise to the defenders of the system, why should they be believed now?

We need more scepticism (not more cynicism); we need class politics (not a retreat from it); and we need a vigorous opposition that ensures exposure is followed by action.

This is not to propose the left's return to the bad old days of half-baked jargon masquerading as Marxism but to suggest a cool, clear look at the way things are in the country.

The left should stop making excuses for itself and others in positions of power and influence – in politics, business, the media and the law – who act in the interests of rich minorities, seldom for the common good, never for the help of the unpopular minorities. Labour should propose and promote constitutional change, to remove the present supremacy of property rights, so often an excuse for the failure of politicians to defend or promote the public interest.

Has the Whitaker committee's report on the Constitution died of political malnutrition?

Twenty-five years ago, the Kenny Report proposed a course that would have helped local authorities to acquire the land they needed for houses.

The report was welcomed all round until the men of property got at the parties and the parties threw up their hands in horror: devotion to the Constitution prevented them from doing what the committee proposed.

What are we left with? A whimper from Bacon, a growl from the market and a growing number of people on the streets.

There are those who bridle at any hint of State intervention or regulation in any shape or form. It's a burden, they say, imposed by begrudgers on the enterprising.

This means, wink and nod, that skulduggery is essential to efficiency. It's not: the countries of northern Europe that are most efficient are also those where regulation is strongest. Cronyism is the enemy of enterprise, masquerading as its friend.

Labour should leave no doubt where it stands on immigration and the reduction of debt among developing countries, as well as the demand for the promised referendum on membership of Partnership for Peace. The party wants to provide sound social-democratic government. It should begin by getting down to full-blooded, unequivocal opposition.

Lynch's career raises no blushes

THEY'LL BURY Jack Lynch in Cork today and honour the last Fianna Fáil leader over whose career no doubts are raised.

The irony can scarcely have been lost on those who spoke well of him this week, when tributes to Lynch's public service competed for attention with reports from the tribunals over which judges Moriarty and Flood preside.

For among the many who praised him were several who had contributed, for better or worse, to the events that have changed Fianna Fáil and the country since his arrival as leader and Taoiseach 33 years ago.

The party was already changing then, and Lynch continued the slow march towards modernisation which had begun with Seán Lemass – and the coalition governments he opposed.

When Lynch retired in 1979, the nature as well as the style of leadership changed; and, because of the importance of leadership in Fianna Fáil, so did the party.

His replacement was the first jolt in what was to become a headlong decline.

The party Lynch joined was populist in the classic sense: more movement than party, convinced that it embodied the spirit of the nation, from which its own ideals were both inseparable and indistinguishable.

The ideals were not expressed in political programmes, but in broad aspirations favouring unity, the Irish language and life on the land; to which the programmes for economic expansion had lately been added.

If the party didn't need written programmes, it was because policy on every important issue was articulated by the leader; the party seldom doubted his word and always followed his line.

This made leadership more important and the leader more powerful than in an orthodox party: Éamon de Valera and Seán Lemass were remote, unquestioned, all but untouchable.

And if Jack Lynch could be called a reluctant leader, it was because that was the kind of daemonic leadership – Dev had been elevated to the status of a demi-god – which he did not want.

High-flown rhetoric was not his style. He never cared for notions of a golden age, especially one that existed only in the imaginations of Charles Kickham and Dev.

He followed Lemass' lead on the need for reconciliation, North and South: he thought political division bred in the Civil War or in sectarian hostility as damaging to democracy as the violence which he loathed in any shape or form.

By the time he quit its leadership, Fianna Fáil was beginning to be a different, more orthodox, more modern party, capable of shedding core values when the need arose.

There has been much well-earned praise of his achievements and some fond remembering during the past few days, but a couple of unremarked changes suggest a prescience with which he should be credited.

One was to remove from the Constitution the special position of the Catholic Church, the other was to put a stop to the activities of the party's fund-raising organisation, Taca.

This didn't make him a radical: it showed that he recognised the need to separate Church and State; and that he clearly saw the risks attached to an unhealthy closeness between business and politics.

(His highly successful election campaign in 1969 seemed to include visits to every second convent in the country; and the world tour which took him to Japan was both an effort to secure industry for Cork and Ireland and an advertisement for Gulf Oil.)

By the time he left its leadership, the party stood closer to the rest of Europe, had set relations with the United Kingdom on an even keel (almost) and was less threatening to unionism than some of his colleagues would have it appear.

Lynch did this without moving away from the people he came from or acting as if he needed a change of image or class. He never wanted, never pretended, to be anyone but himself.

A youngish commentator, Jackie Gallagher, of Finlay and Gallagher, marvelled the other night at what he called the innocence of the 1970s. He wondered if tributes, similar to those now awarded to Jack Lynch, would follow his successors.

Barring miracles or sudden, last-minute conversion, it's most unlikely.

In the age of innocence, you see, leaders lived within their means – and ours. They may have forgotten the odd event; but they didn't airbrush all records of meetings, decisions, donations and alliances from their memories.

Their officials didn't rush off to destroy their diaries to protect their bosses' secrets from the enquiring eyes of some independent judge; they didn't have to. No one would dream of claiming that their activities were other than above board.

And the bosses, for their part, were never forced to rely on pathetic variations of Bart Simpson's defence: "I didn't do it, there's no evidence, you can't prove anything."

Jack Lynch was an honourable man, whose name was airbrushed from the party's records after his resignation. Many of his supporters were driven out – Des O'Malley on the grounds of conduct unbecoming – or left.

The nature of the leadership reverted to the old untouchable, unquestioned and unquestioning style; the nature of the party changed with it. Public cynicism grew, not just about Fianna Fáil or its leadership, but (because it suited some to claim there were no distinctions) about politics and politicians at large.

Another enemy of cynicism is being commemorated in Limerick today. Jim Kemmy, socialist, writer, editor and politician, was long committed to the city and the public service of its citizens.

Indeed, he took public service so seriously that he devoted his mayor's allowance to projects that he felt needed the money more than he did.

This country needs the sense of public service demonstrated by a Jack Lynch or a Jim Kemmy, each in his own way; it also needs a calm and resolute approach by those providing public services – often in the teeth of populist opposition and criticism.

The Nursing Alliance has been subjected to a barrage of heavy-handed, in some cases hysterical, criticism for several days.

Indeed, I didn't realise that some of my journalistic colleagues cared so much about the state of the health services – and especially those provided by the public hospitals – until I heard them on the radio.

I can only hope that their interest lasts when the dispute is settled, as it will be, by discussions that should have taken place at least a week ago, if not from the moment of the nurses' overwhelming decision.

In pursuit of the struggle against cynicism, I'd like to encourage people living in Dublin South Central to take a half-an-hour off on Wednesday to vote in the by-election.

It's your choice: if you don't exercise it, you'll have no one to blame but yourself.

Beware of politicians bearing gifts of electoral efficiency

A LFRED AUSTIN WAS writing about his beloved leader, not ours, when he reported, at the turn of another century: "Across the wires the electric message came – 'He is no better, he is much the same.'"

But he might well have had Bertie Ahern, Charlie McCreevy and Mary Harney in mind. We find them as we left them before Christmas – sadly, no better, they are much the same.

Indeed, when officials get around to releasing the State papers for January 2000, I suspect they'll be found under a single heading: Crises Continued.

And anyone who asks "Which crisis?" will be shown a very thick file: Unfinished Business – Housing; Health; Transport; Immigration; Poverty, urban and rural; Environment and Social Affairs.

Imagine some modern Myles na gCopaleen (a pillar of the civil service before he became a columnist in *The Irish Times*) as he dots the *i*s and crosses the *t*s of his new year's summary:

> "Budget a mess. Social partners angry. Public confused. Shannon, as yet undrained, in flood again. Bad news from tribunals; worse feared. Hopes of technology reducing divisions exaggerated. Opposite may be the case."

Quare times. Quare times, indeed, when, in the teeth of a gathering storm, the best the Government can do is to send out Noel Dempsey to run up the flag of electoral reform. What's really wrong with politics, says Noel, is that TDs spend too much time competing with colleagues for votes by doing favours for the public. Not big favours, like appointing them to State boards or finding inside tracks. The kind of clientelism that Noel and the lads object to might help a family find a council house; what helps the builder make a fat profit is something else.

Contractors and financiers prove their patriotism by their contributions to party funds. They don't ask for anything; they don't have to. And to call their dealings clientelism would be, well, crude.

It's like incentives in a way. You incentivise the poor by making it more difficult for them to survive on the dole; the incentives for the rich are to be found in bigger benefits all round.

When the Government wants to help the rich, it's as easy as sticking a line in a finance bill. When it's asked to deal with a social issue, there are complications. For example: house prices go on rising; the numbers of homeless increase; and the McCreevys, Aherns and Harneys would only love to do something about it.

But they're caught between a rock and a hard place. Between the constitutional right to profit from others' need for shelter and obedience to market forces. Somehow, the market forces always win out.

The market also increasingly dictates the way in which health services are organised and operated. That's because here, as in other areas, we move daily closer to the American model in which politicians start by talking about value for money and end with a setup in which money is all that counts.

In the case of electoral reform, Dempsey and his supporters claim the challenges they propose will make for more efficiency and stability without reducing the choice for the electorate or the chances of the smaller parties.

But to reduce the number of deputies from 166 to 100 would not make the system more efficient; it would merely play into the hands of those who want fewer – and weaker – politicians than we have now.

And those who want weaker politicians are, by and large, the very people who sigh at the mention of tribunals, though tribunals are set up precisely because governments take advantage of the weakness of the Dáil.

A parade of scandals has shown that the problems start when ministers feel they don't have to account for themselves and increase when they confuse the public interest with the interests of business friends and contributors to party funds.

One of the ways of putting a stop to this is by increasing the power of the Dáil, which can be done by greater use of committees, following the lead given by the Public Accounts Committee which investigated the DIRT scandal.

Another is by moving more rapidly to the point at which parties won't need financial contributions and anyone found in breach of funding laws is severely penalised. The case is made that there are greater demands on TDs and senators than there were in the 1950s and 1960s. This is so: activity is increasing on the European, Northern and Anglo-Irish fronts. If we wanted to show that we were serious about poverty and exclusion at home or providing help to developing countries, we would have separate committees covering these issues. Committees that ensured they were not forgotten when broader issues were being discussed. But the search for stability is a threadbare excuse for wanting to change the electoral system; so threadbare that the electorate saw through it when it was first used 40 years ago.

The electorate turned it down when it was tried again in a slightly different context seven years later.

As for the list system, it's no help at all to stability. It certainly hasn't worked wonders for Italy, which, at the last count, was between its 56th and 57th government since the war. PR in multi-seat constituencies has served us well and can be improved. But, if anything, we need more, not fewer, politicians, and a tougher, more-powerful parliamentary system.

We need experienced, active, questioning TDs and senators not just to represent an increasing and more diverse population in the old populist sense, but to regulate affairs on behalf of the community as a whole. The Aherns, McCreevys and Harneys, with their associates in industry and finance, and cheerleaders in the media, are intent on making this what they would call a more businesslike place. As far as they're concerned, work-creation is essential to growth and inequality is an inevitable feature of work-creation; redistribution – or any talk of it – is at best a distraction from wealth-creation and at worst its enemy. There is another assumption, to which some Fianna Fáil leaders subscribe – obliquely – and their cheerleaders express more openly, sometimes with a show of bravado.

This is the idea that, on the road to growth, shortcuts may have to be taken; and if that means breaking the law or profiting from an insider track, what of it? (Neither Ahern nor McCreevy saw much wrong with the evasion of DIRT.)

And if the rules are broken with style, as they were by Charles Haughey, what's a forelock-touching hack to do but cheer at the old scrounger's neck?

The Germans, Israelis and Italians are anxious to rid themselves of the legacies of shamed leaders and corrupt practices. Here, there's a growing campaign to rehabilitate someone who hasn't even the dignity to acknowledge his guilt.

Taoiseach gets into hot water over immigrants

O N A ST PATRICK'S Day in the 1970s, one of his friends who met Frank Cluskey on a street in Paris asked what was going on at home. Liam Cosgrave and Oliver J Flanagan were in Rome. Garret FitzGerald was in Washington, Justin Keating in Brussels; their colleagues, like the Wild Geese, were scattered across Europe.

And here was Cluskey strolling in the Champs-Élysées as if he hadn't a care in the world. What was it up to, this Government in exile? "Nothing at all," said Frank, "we're just trying to give the poor little country a chance." Giving this rich little country a chance to be fairer as well as more prosperous is the aim of the Programme of Prosperity and Fairness on which the unions are now voting. Their decision will determine the future of the programme and, it may be, of social partnership. But, for the current Government in exile, other issues reared their heads. On Monday, far away in Australia, Bertie Ahern resumed his struggle with the English language – and the difficult, dangerous issue of immigration.

The Australians appear to have ways of dealing with immigrants from which, the Taoiseach believes, we may learn. A Migration Act provides for mandatory detention of "unlawful non-citizens" who are held in camps while their fate is decided.

It's a system which, despite expert opinion to the contrary, Mr Ahern described as the best integrated in the world. Which caused such a stir – and so much confusion among his supporters – that he was given two opportunities to say that the system would not be introduced here. He didn't take the opportunities, but merely repeated that the Australian system was the best in the world.

At home, his brother Noel Ahern, a TD for Dublin North West, had told *TV3 News* that detention for asylum-seekers was against everything for which Fianna Fáil stood. And Conor Lenihan, a Fianna Fáil TD for Dublin South West, complained repeatedly on *Tonight With Vincent Browne* that the Taoiseach's words had been misinterpreted by the media generally and *The Irish Times* in particular.

"Do you think he knew what he was saying?" Browne asked. "Are you not embarrassed by it?" Lenihan, who wasn't embarrassed, said he was aware of the Australian practice and claimed there were "a lot of similarities between what happens there and ourselves".

One of the other guests on the programme was a Rwandan refugee, John Tambwe, whose father was killed in the plane crash which set off the conflict between the Hutu and Tutsi peoples.

When he explained that, in spite of this, he'd been told by the Irish authorities that he wouldn't be allowed to stay here, Lenihan acknowledged that the Irish system was "not being handled properly".

Browne's question about the Taoiseach understanding refers to Ahern's often ambiguous use of language, which is capable of being interpreted in different ways by different audiences. (The "monstrosity" of Spencer Dock was a case in point.)

Now, though, John Bruton has accused him of playing on the irrational fears of xenophobes who might be persuaded to vote for Fianna Fáil. Ruairí Quinn has challenged his casual assertion that Ireland's refugee application system had been criticised as too liberal by the United Nations High Commission for Refugees.

And Suzanne Egan, one of the authors of a comparative study of refugee law commissioned by the Department of Justice, Equality and Law Reform, said that Ireland would be out of step with most EU states if asylum-seekers were detained here.

As for the Australian system, in 1997, it was found to have breached the International Covenant on Civil and Political Rights – a finding the Australian Government considered "totally unacceptable".

Ahern, however, had moved on by midweek to the United States where countless refugees from hunger and poverty in Ireland and at least one generation of illegal Irish migrants – or "unlawful non-citizens" – found refuge. There, in the enlightened company of Brian Cowen, he could forget such issues as segregation in the Irish camps of the future and the questions that he and Cowen may toss about with John O'Donoghue: should women be kept in Magdalen laundries, as of old? And are the children to be confined to industrial schools? Cowen, on a charm offensive in Washington, has succeeded in appealing to the unionists as he once appealed to the nurses – by showing an exasperating indifference to their case.

The Government had encouraged David Trimble and Gerry Adams to "jump together" in the expectation that devolution would be followed by decommissioning. When it didn't happen and Peter Mandelson suspended the institutions, the Government lurched in the direction of Sinn Féin.

As John Bruton wrote in *The Irish Times* on Wednesday: "When the executive was suspended, the Government (a) refused to accept any responsibility for it, (b) on the record expressed understanding of the decision, and (c) off the record expressed violent anger at it."

If Bruton's view is correct and he seems to have the right air of it – Ahern and Cowen have spent the weeks that followed suspension in a devious realignment with Sinn Féin.

This widens the gap that had begun to appear between the coalition and the opposition, between the Government and the unionists and between the governments in Dublin and London.

Bruton's warning about hollow claims that "the guns are silent" has to be taken seriously. Shootings by republican and loyalist paramilitaries continue; and bombs, like that found this week, are still being prepared.

Ahern once said the people who supported the Belfast Agreement did not vote for an armed peace. He was right. But most of the IRA's weapons are hidden in this State, and the danger of another Omagh persists.

The last thing that's needed is another round of ambiguous rhetoric by Ahern as if he were trying to mollify a *cumann* down the road.

Conor Lenihan was trying to mollify a different audience at a function of the Irish Association of Corporate Treasurers in Dublin last week.

> "My overarching theme," he said, according to his script, "is that it would be a great shame if, as a result of the tribunals... and DIRT inquiries, we moved... from a position of relative non-compliance to a culture of 'over-compliance' and 'over-regulation' of our economy...

> "An over-anxiety to secure full, retrospective, documentary compliance in relation to offshore accounts based at the International Financial Services Centre is not a good signal to international investors, and dare I say it was never the intention of the PAC inquiry into this matter."

Conor Lenihan is a member of the Public Accounts Committee.

APRIL 29th, 2000

Government's handling of immigration inept

THE UNITED STATES was in the depths of depression when Franklin D Roosevelt declared, in his inaugural speech, that "the only thing we have to fear is fear itself".

It was a belief famously repeated almost 30 years later by John F Kennedy, in the context of a different but no less ominous challenge. Now, in another time and place, it might well apply to those who are worried about the arrival of asylum-seekers in cities, towns and villages around the State.

But, in our case and in these days, fear is complicated by an absence of leadership and the ineptitude of the Department of Justice.

Of course, there are bound to be problems when strangers are set down in what must seem isolated places without work or the opportunity to earn a living.

Their isolation is increased by inadequate transport, difficult access to services and a mere £15 a week to cover expenses other than food and shelter.

But refugees (whatever they are called and for whatever reason they come) have never fared well in this State.

The first group that I can remember were the Hungarians who arrived here soon after the rising in Budapest in 1956. To us, they were victims of a communist regime and, therefore, heroic.

Though Ireland may have been neutral, its citizens generally were not; and at Shannon Airport great crowds turned out to give them a rousing Cold War welcome.

They were housed in east Clare in an old army camp at Knockalisheen. It was a bleak place surrounded by a barbed-wire fence; for a time, people came to stand outside to stare at the Nissen huts and their silent occupants.

We were shocked when they began to complain about the poor heating, the quality of the food, the absence of work and the restrictions on their movements.

Limerick was a less-welcoming place then; and when a few of them got drunk and ended up in court, they were told they had abused the hospitality the city had shown them.

Within months they went on hunger strike, partly in protest against their conditions and partly because they felt that, if work wasn't available in Ireland, they should be allowed to go to Canada where they would have no difficulty finding jobs.

When they had gone, they were remembered with an air of

puzzlement. There was a feeling that, as refugees, they ought to have been grateful for what they'd been given. They had no right to ask for better conditions or to want jobs in Canada.

Not to put too fine a point on it, we thought of the Hungarians who came to Ireland as having fewer rights than we had and little or no ability to decide their future.

When the Dáil debated the events at Knockalisheen, most of those who spoke hinted at the ingratitude of the refugees and only one, Jack McQuillan, suggested that it was our attitude to them which was at fault.

Ireland was a poor country in the 1950s. We had not gained from the post-war boom which had enhanced the economies of western Europe; indeed, we were suffering the most serious drop in population since the Famine.

Now that our circumstances have changed, have our attitudes to less fortunate people changed, too? Have we developed a deeper understanding of the needs of those who must quit their homes and homelands?

Or do we still think of them as we did in the 1950s, though we are immeasurably better off than we were then and we have a capacity to be generous and imaginative which we could scarcely have dreamed of 45 years ago?

The President, Mrs McAleese, favours the generous and imaginative way. So did her predecessor, Mary Robinson. And Mrs Robinson's predecessor, Paddy Hillery, speaks pointedly of the wealth that we have accumulated but failed to distribute.

The Catholic bishops have this week called for a compassionate and welcoming attitude to asylum-seekers and refugees and suggested that those already here be accepted and allowed to work.

Reports have come from different parts of the country which tell of a priest here, a woman there, taking a stand against suspicion and fear.

In Corofin, a village on the edge of the Burren, a man called Declan Kelleher agrees to take the chair at a potentially difficult meeting on condition that "not one prejudicial remark [is] passed by anybody".

And he asks his audience: "Is there one person in this hall that did not… have an ancestor in the last century who was an economic refugee? It is very, very important that that is remembered."

But there are doubts and fears which give rise to demands, like that raised at Clogheen, Co. Tipperary, that arrivals should be screened for Aids or should have their records checked.

At Clogheen, the Vee Valley Hotel, where asylum-seekers are to be accommodated, was set on fire; and in Ballsbridge, Dublin, residents have asked the High Court to quash a Government decision to use a guesthouse as a reception centre.

Fears are fanned by reports like that published across eight columns in the *Irish Independent* on March 18th under the heading "Refugee racket fears as 43 arrivals demand asylum".

It began: "Fears were mounting last night that an organised immigration racket was targeting Ireland after 43 people of mixed nationality walked off a boat yesterday and sought political asylum."

Reading the accounts of local meetings and listening to the debates admirably chaired by Rodney Rice this week, it would appear that – with a few lurid exceptions – the most common complaints are about the absence of information.

But, then, the Department of Justice is one of the most forbidding and secretive institutions in the State; a department in which openness is not so much welcomed as suffered by those at its head and in all probability by many who work in it.

The most serious complaint is of a complete absence of leadership by John O'Donoghue and his colleagues in Government.

There is no sense that this is a human issue, reflecting one of the great human issues of our time. "It's a question of implementing the law of the land," O'Donoghue said flatly.

Is it any wonder that almost 60 per cent of those questioned in the latest *Irish Times*/MRBI poll should have said the Government was handling the issue not particularly well or not well at all?

MAY 6th, 2000

Racism turns the republican ideal on its head

"WE'VE DONE OUR bit," said my father-in-law Frank Kelly, an old republican. "We made sure the Irish could run their own show. What those who come after us make of the country is up to them."

I was reminded of his expectations the other day when Seán Ó Mordha wrote to me about reaction to his immensely popular story of the Irish State, *Seven Ages*.

"One thing came through in all the letters from viewers," he said. "They know they have a State and they are citizens and can still decide their destiny. All is not lost." My father-in-law didn't talk about it in a sentimental way or, as some of the old comrades did, as if life stood still once the fighting ended. He took much of what followed with the phlegmatic air of a born Londoner.

Because of his matter-of-fact attitude, his accounts of what happened usually steered clear of heroics and high drama. Yes, he agreed, it would have been better if James Connolly's had been the dominant voice in 1916. But it wasn't, so a social and economic revolution was out of the question.

The comrades who believed that life stood still took power and held on too long. The changes, as Connolly had feared, had more to do with the colour of flags and letter boxes than with the nature of society.

The more idealistic went on believing in a republic of fierce

227

independence, egalitarian leanings and international alliances reflecting Ireland's leadership in a changing world.

As for the later generations: there have been successes which can be set to the credit of politicians, public servants and our pragmatic combination of public and private enterprise, native and foreign.

Our course has been erratic, from the self-inflicted damage of civil war through hopeless decades to unimagined prosperity. And most are impressed by the success, as is clear from the levels of satisfaction with the Government.

But something is missing here, an absence simply noted by puzzled commentators who ask, "Why aren't we happy?", as they wander on to the next dizzy celebration.

It may be that we (or enough of us to make a difference) haven't had much to do with the growth of prosperity, have only the vaguest hope of sharing in it and have little or no idea where we go from here.

The unease isn't confined to bus and train drivers. It's felt by doctors, nurses and teachers; by those who share Liz McManus' conviction about the health service we could (but do not) have; by everyone who worries about the housing crisis.

The level of undecided respondents in *Irish Times*/MRBI polls gives some indication of attitudes to politics, though not the whole story.

But if only one in five, as the poll shows, failed to turn out, electoral politics would be in a healthy state. The real rate of abstention is much higher: in the 1997 general election it was more than one in three.

And those least likely to vote are the 18–24 year olds. In the latest poll, almost 30 per cent of them are among the undecided, which could mean that as many as half won't turn out next time.

We have happily exchanged a degree of sovereignty for membership of the European Union and entered a new relationship with the United Kingdom in the hope of achieving a durable settlement in Northern Ireland.

It's in our domestic affairs that real dissatisfaction has been generated. The sense of ownership which Frank Kelly and his comrades assumed would flow from the establishment of the new state has diminished.

The ownership they hoped for would not have been exclusive. It would not have been confined to one class or centre of power. It would have been open and accountable and it would have informed our attitudes to our communal property, culture and the environment.

If this sense of ownership had existed we would have been more confident and more at ease in our attitudes to immigrants. The feeling that we protect "our own" by attacking some of the most vulnerable people in the world turns the republican ideal on its head.

The republicans of Frank's generation built fragile alliances with the Soviet Union and with an incipient nationalist movement in Egypt. They took courage from events in South Africa and the poems of Walt Whitman. Connolly was a member of the Wobblies, the International Workers of the World.

Those who rage about "our own" are often those who have never lifted a finger or raised a voice in defence of Travellers, the homeless, the old, the ill or the unemployed. Their concern would be more convincing if, indeed, it started at home. It's the consistency of their records that makes more convincing the leadership of a Michael D Higgins, a Pat Rabbitte or a Des Geraghty.

On socio-economic issues, Church leaders such as the bishops Willie Walsh and Walton Empey are, as usual, imaginative and humane. And the Sean Healys, Stanislaus Kennedys and Peter McVerrys fight on and on and on.

Fianna Fáil and Fine Gael are on a slow bicycle race to reform, anxious not to disturb their most backward supporters but hoping not to be shown up as unwilling or unable to change.

Bertie Ahern chose the annual Fianna Fáil outing to Arbour Hill as the venue for his latest denial and assertion of straight dealing. The denial didn't convince the public: in a *Sunday Independent*/IMS Poll, 46 per cent said they didn't believe him, and Fianna Fáil's support has dropped four points since February.

But Ahern went further and claimed ownership of the tribunals:

> "I was the Taoiseach that set up these tribunals, nobody else. I and my Government colleagues set up these tribunals along with our colleagues, the Progressive Democrats and Mary Harney…"

Balderdash. The Oireachtas decides when and on what terms tribunals are established. And it is to the Oireachtas that the tribunals report. Ahern fought tooth and nail against including the Ansbacher accounts in one case and Ray Burke's affairs in another.

But amnesia is a terrible thing – and it's contagious. Dermot Ahern says he doesn't know how much the trade unions contribute to the Labour Party. He could have looked up the published accounts: the total for 1999 was £36,309. Sure he'd lose it in a tot.

And one of the officials in Peter Mandelson's entourage has discovered that Brian Cowen's argument on the North is "presented with all the subtlety and open-mindedness that one would expect from a member of Sinn Féin".

Really? As open-minded as that?

Vulnerable in society still waiting for answers to questions on prosperity of lopsided State

BERTIE AHERN'S WARNING from afar about an economic downturn raises questions that were first asked when the period of prosperity began in the mid-1990s but have not been satisfactorily answered since.

I once tried putting these questions – about the origins of our extraordinary growth, who benefits most from it and what happens if and when the downturn comes – to Charlie McCreevy. But he was too busy claiming victory over his critics to explain how it was done.

And an economist whom I've known for years was even more baffling when he dismissed any and every criticism of the way we are with the counterclaim that it was simply inspired by the spite and jealousy of the left.

The left, he said, would like nothing better than to be able to report the collapse of every enterprise, the failure of every investment, the bankruptcy of every profitable industry – home-grown or foreign – and the overwhelming growth of dole queues in every quarter.

I tried reminding him of an old acquaintance in London, a man who'd astonished the company one comradely evening by refusing to drink to the collapse of the system. He was older than the rest of us and he'd been through the mill: left unemployed and hopeless after the First World War and homeless in the 1930s. Whenever the system collapsed, Bill and his friends were under it, at the bottom of the pile.

Now, in another country and another century, we are once more perched between success and failure with uncertainty growing daily about the side on which our chips will fall. Report after report sings the praises of an economy that has not only thrown off the shackles of its own past but avoided the pitfalls in which others now stumble.

And, even before Ahern sent his characteristically vague message from Brazil, report after report had warned those who didn't already feel it in their bones that this was a crazily lopsided society in which too many people were left undefended by the State – the only body capable of defending them.

It was at the meeting convened by the Irish Autism Alliance to discuss the Jamie Sinnott case in HQ/Irish Music Hall of Fame on Tuesday that the vulnerability of so many in such a lopsided society struck me.

Here were people like Jamie Sinnott's mother Kathryn, dedicated and determined; campaigners like Seamus Greene, with an eye on the political edge; and up to 1,000 others representing the handicapped of every kind and in every way.

People who had for so long been told that society couldn't afford education, care or other services. People who'd been fobbed off with lies and bland excuses, not only by politicians but by officials practised in the art of dismissal – who had learned to blind themselves to people's needs for the sake of a few pounds.

But those for whom autism is the primary concern should take the advice given by a seasoned campaigner on Tuesday. He shrewdly observed that the worst position they could adopt would be to stand alone and find themselves in isolation.

Were they to stand alone they'd be picked off, one by one, by political cynics or their officials.

Parents would be told that what was on offer was all the Government could afford. If everybody's needs were met – certainly the wider needs of handicap, not only in education but in health and care – the State would be bankrupt.

You may have noticed that the spectre of bankruptcy is often raised in some quarters, as a rule by the same smart-aleck commentators, to make a case against meeting the community's obligations to the less well off – never to block payments to the rich and super-rich.

It's the kind of rubbish vulnerable, generous and considerate people have been sold for years. They're urged to think of ever-increasing taxes on the assumption that the burden is borne by people like themselves.

The trouble is that this is partly true. The burden is disproportionately borne by people like themselves. They pay when public money – their money – is spent on public services.

And they pay when public money – their money – is not spent on public services, of which they and their poorer neighbours are most in need.

The lopsided imposition of tax and the even greater discrepancy in need are accepted as a law of nature.

Simply stated, those who ought to be paying their way pay as little as possible. And they get away with it because politicians and banks connive with them and suited ranks of accountants, lawyers, tax consultants and sundry corporate advisers work for them.

Some are the 21st century's absentee landlords or are in companies up to their necks in transfer pricing or double-crossing their own governments by taking advantage of the schemes obligingly laid on by Cayman Ireland.

And while the absentee landlords and their foreign counterparts are served by an army of well-schooled lackeys, who do we have to look after our interests? As often as not, a pack of fumblers to whom you wouldn't lend a fiver at a poker school on a Friday night.

To hell with rights: the Exchequer comes first

POLITICIANS AND COMMENTATORS share a fondness for subjects which can be summed up in a slogan and lend themselves to tidy conclusions. The trouble with the health service, especially for politicians, is that it's all too easily understood – especially by those who have most need of it – but impossible to tidy up for popular consumption.

No one is too old, too young or too remote from everyday life to be unaware of the truth that health cuts hurt the old, the sick and the handicapped. It makes the undeniable connection between health and public funding: that's why Fianna Fáil once chose it as an election slogan.

Of course politicians of all shades also acknowledge the truism that you can't solve the problems of health, or any other service, simply by throwing money at them. Not that that was ever likely, even in the richest little country in Europe.

Still, the richest country with the poorest health service in the European Union was a shameful record that must somehow be erased. And until the other day friends, foes and commentators were convinced that this was the Government with the means and the incentive to do it.

The Fianna Fáil–Progressive Democrats Coalition had spent four years living with the issue. It had been told time and again what was wrong with the service – not only by political opponents like Liz McManus, Gay Mitchell and John Gormley, but by nurses, doctors and civil servants.

So it knew what was wrong and what might be done to change it. The remedy it chose was the most cautious on offer, its presentation by Micheál Martin the glossiest that could be devised by numerous advisers and public relations consultants, not to mention the political skills of some of the wiliest in the business.

Then, in an act of deliberate meanness, it postponed until 2003 the extension of the medical card scheme to 200,000 people cruelly trapped above the present income limit of around £5,000 (€6,348) a year.

Suddenly it was clear that what the coalition was trying to do was not to reform the health service – certainly not to attempt anything radical – but to win the next general election. After all, not only the estimable Jack Jones of MRBI (whose book *In Your Opinion* has just been published) but every researcher in the field had identified health as the outstanding issue for the electorate. The issue to be tackled if the election was to be won.

Health, however, does not stand alone: it's inextricably bound to other issues, not least the yawning gaps between rich and poor.

You don't need a procession of researchers to tell you that the poor live shorter and less comfortable lives than the rest of the population. You don't need to be reminded by the Economic and Social Research Institute, the Combat Poverty Agency, the Conference of Religious in Ireland and the St Vincent de Paul Society that the poor suffer most from inadequate education, housing and public transport.

(On housing alone, there were messages this week from Sister Stanislaus Kennedy of Focus – calling on 40,000 people to sign cards representing the shortfall in local authority and voluntary housing – and from a group of artists and activists in Bray with their exhibition, No Fixed Abode.) As Ray Dooley of the Children's Rights Alliance said: "Study after study has shown the link between poverty and health." The doctors know. The nurses know. The officials of the Department of Health who famously met ministers at Ballymascanlon seemed to know. How the hell could members of the Government not know?

How many shared the rage of James O'Reilly of the Irish Medical Organisation when he heard that the Government was either unaware of the link between health and poverty or coldly ignoring it? I remembered how, many years ago, I listened to a poor man tell his wife to sell the last of their cattle to pay for his stay in a nursing home and the injury that cost him the sight of one eye. When the time came, they left Ennis on the west Clare train and, from Miltown Malbay, sick as he was, trudged the last few miles home.

They told us then that we couldn't afford a decent service. And now? Reading the report of the task force set up as a result of Jamie Sinnott's case, I am reminded of the official response to the report on equal citizenship (and disability) published in December 1999. It said:

"The Department of Finance cannot accept these recommendations which imply the underpinning by law of access to and provision of services for people with disability as a right.

"This right, if given a statutory basis, would be prohibitively expensive for the Exchequer and could lead to requests from other persons seeking access to health and other services without regard to the eventual cost of providing these services."

To hell with your rights: the Exchequer comes first.

Progressive Democrats fail to live up to their own expectations

"WE WILL NOT mortgage the country's future with costly promises," said Mary Harney at the Progressive Democrats' annual conference in Limerick last weekend.

And, as if it clinched the argument, "we believe in Government, not gambling". She was cheered to the rafters. After five years in Government with the old enemy, the Progressive Democrats were no longer radical; they were certainly not redundant. Watching the show on television, it seemed that not the slightest doubt crossed the mind of any of them.

But on her way to Limerick, the Tánaiste had glided through McCreevyland, the territory of her own best buddie Charlie, a Minister for Finance known far and wide as the gamblers' friend.

Even as she spoke, his followers were celebrating his latest coup – a tax break smuggled into the Finance Bill designed to crown the careers of professional sportspeople with a pot of gold.

Not any old sportspeople, of course, but the *crème de la crème*, the elite who'd already made it to the top. They mightn't need the loot; all the more reason to pile it on: McCreevy was never one to take need into account.

And if there were complaints – say, in the ranks of the GAA or among those who'd lobbied, with poor results, on behalf of the homeless or the disabled – what of it? It wouldn't be the first time McCreevy had kicked sand in the faces of those who felt entitled to a share of the community's resources.

As for the Progressive Democrats, they'd never been known to worry if those who had much were given more.

On the contrary. What-we-have-we-hold was the theme of their weekend. And it will be the theme of both Michael McDowell's presidency and the party's campaign in the general election.

"The country can't afford a lurch to the left," said Harney. McDowell spoke of Labour in Government as "disastrous madness".

And, in debate with Derek McDowell of Labour on the *News at One*, he was more specific: a Blairite party would be acceptable. What we had here, though, were the "same old ideological people" as before.

This is the heart of the matter: the Progressive Democrats are determined, not only to dictate the terms on which the next general election is fought, but how the issues are defined.

There was a time when ideology was a term invariably applied to the left and then qualified by the term "alien".

The threat of "an alien ideology" sent well-heeled citizens scuttling off to search, on bended knees, for reds under their beds.

The new ideology comes from the right. It's for the well-heeled, the what-we-have-we-hold crowd, whose political spokesmen are the Progressive Democrats. Their reverse takeover of Fianna Fáil was achieved without a fuss.

From lofty perches they pontificate on the affairs of what they call the real world. As one of the right's favourite economists, Moore McDowell, told the broadcaster Joe Duffy last week: "You are paid to emote, I am paid to think." And when the likes of Mary Harney or Michael McDowell pontificate from their perches, it behoves the rest of us to sit up and take notice. Otherwise we're apt to get the wrong end of the stick.

For instance, when Harney talks about gamblers, she's not talking about McCreevy's friends, whether in the members' enclosure at the Curragh or hoovering up the benefits of a 50 per cent cut in capital gains tax.

What the Progressive Democrats consider potentially disastrous is the kind of promise made by the Labour Party and the modest reforms that even Fine Gael considers essential to the development of a just society.

As Labour's McDowell, Derek, puts it, his party wants to achieve "tangible and measurable improvements in the public services". More to the point, it wouldn't just talk about it, it would get down to improving health, housing and education and reducing the gap between rich and poor.

And, yes, it would cost money – but the money would not be found by raising personal taxes. Which is still not enough for the Progressive Democrats who have to be reminded by that honourable old curmudgeon Des O'Malley how they've failed to live up to their own expectations on public spending.

They've failed to live up to their own expectations on other issues as well. They once talked of refusing to have a referendum on abortion until consensus had been achieved.

It hasn't been achieved, not even in their own small party.

Consensus was never going to be achieved and everybody with a titter of political wit knew it. But Bertie Ahern, who likes to go a step of the road with everyone, had made a promise… and Harney bit her lip and agreed.

Ahern called for a calm debate and ended up screeching at the opposition in the Dáil while his henchmen – Frank Fahey and Dick Roche, for example – set out to spread muck like farmers spreading slurry in the fields of the West.

Harney, who last week prated about gambling, now expects the electorate to take a gamble in one of its most serious decisions without the information it should have had: the booklet the Referendum Commission produced will not have been delivered to the homes of most of those who have votes. The text on which they vote will not be on their polling cards.

But expecting people to play blind-man's buff on March 6th is all of a piece with the hypocrisy, cynicism and confusion which have characterised the Government's attitude to the issue from the start.

They needn't worry: hospitals in Britain will terminate the pregnancies of 7,000 Irishwomen this year as they've done every year since the 1983 referendum passed.

Those who suffer most, as usual, will be those who are too poor or too frightened to travel. Women who ought to be able to avail of a properly supervised and conducted medical service at home.

Michael Noonan is right: this is the worst Government we've had to endure.

JULY 6th, 2002

Fianna Fáil is heading blithely into big trouble, as it did after 1977 election

IT WAS A very wet year in 1979. But similarities with conditions in 2002 don't stop there. The Government elected in 1977 had the biggest majority and the most popular Taoiseach in the history of the State. Jack Lynch was to be described – by his long-time opponent Liam Cosgrave – as the most popular politician since Daniel O'Connell.

Fianna Fáil was in better shape than it had ever been. With luck, it seemed, the party would be in office for two, three or four terms, maybe until the turn of the century.

There were some obvious snags. One was the size of the majority: it was big enough to allow opposition to the leadership to fester and grow on the back benches. Then, the manifesto on which the historic majority had been won was founded on a questionable premise: that it was possible to spend our way out of recession.

So the Government had embarked on a spectacular programme designed to encourage spending by promoting growth and employment. The programme's most striking features were the abolition of rates on houses and a dramatic reduction in road tax on cars. These, we were told, were the pump-priming measures the economy needed.

Two years later, it was beginning to dawn on us that the manifesto hadn't worked. And, to make matters worse, Ireland had been hit, for the second time in seven years, by a paralysing international oil crisis.

I wrote about it here in a piece which began:

"On the third and final day of summer it rained. But that was the least of the Government's worries in the Land of Nod. Oil supplies were running short, both at home and in the streets, which left the citizens cold and bad-tempered. Fights had broken out where they queued to fill their cars with petrol.

"The post was no longer delivered and hadn't been for months, because the people who used to deliver it refused to go on starving on the wages the Government paid.

"The telephones, which had never worked well, had ceased to ring altogether in many parts of the country. Some said this might have been just as well, since it stopped the spread of bad news. And none of the news was good in the Land of Nod on the third and final day of summer, especially for the Government."

The worst, as the Cabinet was about to hear, was not the queues at the filling stations or the sound of public services grinding to a halt; it was the news that the State now had two chiefs of police. This was because the Supreme Court had decided that the Government's attempt to fire the old garda commissioner was unconstitutional. To make matters worse, the new man was already in office.

But, as it happened, this bizarre turn of events simply confirmed that, when things start to go wrong for a party or government, there's no knowing where the rot will stop. And in the wintry summer of 1979 the rot had already set in.

The Government lost heavily in the European elections and was soon to lose two critical by-elections in Cork. The ministers who were closest to Lynch advised him to resign and, when he did, they lost the leadership. Charles Haughey was leader and Taoiseach by the end of the year.

The reign which led directly or indirectly to the McCracken, Moriarty and Flood tribunals and to the Ansbacher and DIRT inquiries had begun. Some who look to the United States and the scandals of Enron, WorldCom, Xerox and Arthur Andersen say it couldn't happen in this State. And in a sense it's true: we do things differently here.

John Kenneth Galbraith, interviewed lately in the London *Independent*, attributed the American problem in part to corporations which had grown so complex that they were almost beyond monitoring. (The interview was reproduced in the *Irish Independent* on Thursday.) The corporations, said Galbraith, "have grown out of effective control by the owners, the stockholders, into nearly absolute control by the management and the individuals recruited by management".

Management, in turn, had set its own rewards at fantastic levels: such was their power that until they carried their behaviour to extremes and the companies collapsed "there was almost no complaint from the shareholders – the owners".

In this State, scandals have followed a different course: political cover is provided for certain owners and controllers of big business (usually home-grown) when they choose to break the law or act as if it didn't apply to them. This was what lay at the rotten core of Ansbacher. Des Traynor was able to operate an illegal bank from the offices of CRH because he was Haughey's adviser and Haughey availed of its services. Others well known in politics and business followed his example.

As certain businessmen, politicians and accountants still insist, tax evasion and breach of exchange were taken for granted. They followed the patterns set by the political and business leadership. They were part of the culture of the time.

So were the failures of the regulatory system and the rampant hypocrisy of those who preached austerity for those who couldn't escape taxation but connived at the fraudulent practices of those who could. The crooked accountants and lawyers aren't all in the US.

Looking back, it would be wrong to exaggerate the comparisons between 1979 and 2002. But it would be foolish to pretend that the Fianna Fáil–Progressive Democrat appeal to the electorate this year was not as dodgy as the manifesto of 1977. Bertie Ahern and Charlie McCreevy were among the TDs swept into the Dáil in 1977. Ahern was to become Haughey's chief whip and favourite son. McCreevy, like the newly nominated senator Mary Harney, joined the resolute anti-Haugheyites inside the party until she left to found the Progressive Democrats.

But when the profligacy of the 1970s led inevitably to the crippling of the public services after 1987, McCreevy was the man who cut the welfare services.

And where were Ahern and McCreevy this week? McCreevy was burbling on about miracles, and Ahern, pint in hand, was opening a pub. The sound around them was of chickens coming home to roost.

Ironic twists in economy that threaten famine

I WAS BEGINNING to think we had lost our gift for irony and contradiction when the President appeared on television the other night admiring a famine house that had been rebuilt in New York.

The builders had used stones collected from ruined houses of the 1840s and, as Carole Coleman reported on RTÉ's evening news, their work was much admired by Mrs McAleese and others who thought it a moving tribute to those whom hunger had driven from home.

The irony lay not in the President's sensitive approach but in the Government's response on the same day to migrants seeking refuge and work on these shores. Michael McDowell had put it tartly in an article in the *Sunday Independent*: "Ireland simply cannot invite the huddled masses of the world to migrate here at will. It is... the business of government to decide in accordance with law who is admitted to live in Ireland and who is not."

So McDowell chose to forget not only those who left in the 19th century but the procession of political leaders who pleaded in Washington for our own (white and English-speaking) illegals during the last 20 years.

And the gardaí came for the Nigerians and Romanians in Dublin on Tuesday morning as they will come for others elsewhere in the State for as long as the present policy persists.

The Fianna Fáil–Progressive Democrat Coalition is accused of spreading fear and alarm – in spite of efforts at reassurance. Integrating Ireland, the network of refugee, asylum-seeker and immigrant support groups, said the extent, secrecy and lack of due process in this week's operations raised serious concern.

But there have been too many reports and threats of action in too many areas for any suggestion of cutbacks or job losses to be taken lightly. And, with monotonous predictability, the blows fall where they are most bitterly felt.

Miriam Donohoe reported here on Thursday that the recruitment of 800 staff to the health services had been "put on hold". Micheál Martin doesn't want this to be described as a cutback. The same applies to Tom Kitt and the reduction of €32 million in the allocation of aid to the poorest of the world's poor.

Kitt's fumbling explanation that the reduction in aid wasn't really a cut was interrupted by a growl from David Hanly on *Morning Ireland*: "When did the Minister for Finance discover the downturn in the economy?" This is the downturn which has caused the ceiling for the drugs refund scheme and the cost of attending accident and emergency departments to be raised – risking the health of the poorest of the Irish poor, as Liz McManus points out.

It is the downturn which is raising the cost of third-level education, disrupting services at hospitals from Monaghan to Loughlinstown and causing havoc wherever citizens depend on the State.

All of which happens under the noses of ministers – including Miracle Man McCreevy himself – but they take not a blind bit of notice. Some are too busy elsewhere: on July 5th, we reported on McDowell at the Garda Depot in Templemore, telling recruits that the Government was seeking an increase of 50 per cent (from 8,000 to 12,000) in the number of people charged with drug offences in the next six years.

His aim is to achieve a 25 per cent increase in drug seizures by 2004, and an increase of 50 per cent by 2008. It sounds as if it ought to be index-linked. And if the target isn't met, what other section of the community will get it in the neck? But McDowell is not the only Minister to be surrounded by thickets of confusion. Bertie Ahern was always a hopeless case: his only function in the election campaign was to smile, shake hands and shut up.

All this while Charlie McCreevy and Mary Harney sorted things out and left P J Mara or one of his friends to deal with Rupert Murdoch, Tony O'Reilly and lesser fry in the media on Fianna Fáil's behalf.

In theory, all Ahern had to do was to stay out of trouble and hope that McCreevy in particular knew what he was doing. And what he did was to go on peddling investment at knockdown prices (the lowest corporate taxes in the EU), discourage regulation and promote freedom of movement – financial, of course.

Essentially, it was handing control to corporations – a few Irish, some European, but mostly American – and trusting in the system.

There were two flaws in the scheme: first, the system didn't always work as it was meant to; second, whatever about a corporation, a government and a state could not be allowed to run on automatic pilot.

Indeed, when I wrote about the imminence of hard times in the past, some were convinced that I looked forward to the collapse of the system or to some capitalists of my acquaintance getting their comeuppance.

But, although I have little time for the more ebullient advocates of capitalism, my expectations are modest. I keep remembering a friend in London who was disappointed when an old neighbour of ours, who'd had the worst of things for a very long time, confessed that he didn't share our delight at the prospect of a collapse of capitalism.

The reasons were obvious: whenever, in his long life, the system had crashed – and it had happened often enough – he and his neighbours had found themselves under the wreckage.

So we'd better make the best of what we've got by reform and regulation. It's a conclusion that some gurus of the American way have already reached.

And finally: the market won't solve everything

THIS WEEK, AS we celebrate the clear result of the referendum on the Treaty of Nice and look forward to inquiries into the baleful effects of the Catholic Church's secretive ways, the following question occurs to me: do we always have to wait until our backs are to the wall before we engage in open, whole-hearted debate and arrive at definite conclusions?

Of course we don't but, looking at our record, we can't avoid the conclusion that waiting until decisions and action are forced on us is one of our less-endearing habits.

It was so when I started work as a reporter in the *Clare Champion*. It remains so as I write this final column almost half a century later.

Dammit, there have been times when it almost proved fatal. And among the reasons for it was that we had a convenient excuse for our failures in history: the 800 years of oppression allowed us to blame others for what was still amiss 30 years after independence.

Of course dominance by Britain had helped to retard our development. But, by the middle of the last century, so had the idea that we could survive economically on our own: a notion, by the way, which ran counter to the doctrine of interdependence preached by Éamon de Valera as leader of the League of Nations in the 1930s.

After the war, the idea persisted that we could survive, not only in isolation but as a largely rural society and determined to remain so. This was absurd, but we made a virtue of short-sightedness even when the signs of doom crowded every railway station and clogged every port.

We waited until the last minute to question the orthodoxy of self-sufficiency and isolation because to do so earlier would have been unpatriotic or, as we feared in our superstitious way, might bring the whole house of cards down around us.

In any event, there was another choice, an alternative to emigration but more fatalistic.

Among the 100,000 or so who marched through Dublin and Limerick in IRA man Seán South's funeral were several Fianna Fáil TDs.

Like the rest of us who took part, they probably had no idea where we were going or what we might do when we got there; we were looking for emotional release. (I wrote about South's "murder".) For a society dying on its feet it was, ironically, a safety valve.

And it was not until I worked in Belfast – for the *Irish Press* in 1959 – that I began to have the faintest idea what our great demonstration meant to people of "the other persuasion" as they were called by a character in Joyce's masterly story, 'The Dead'. Those of "the other persuasion" were people whose ways were a mystery to us in the 1950s and 1960s. But so were the ways of the hierarchy.

Indeed, if the orthodoxy of nationalism and the caesura drawn across Southern society by the Civil War distorted debate and inhibited development, the silence and secrecy imposed by the Catholic authorities left deeper and more lasting scars.

Remarkably, the change in policy which favoured industrial development and foreign investment provoked less debate than the changes promised by the Second Vatican Council which might have given the laity a sense of shared ownership in their Church.

I had long before ceased to feel any attachment to Catholicism, though John Horgan's reports from Rome during the Vatican Council were fascinating.

And no one with a spark of intellectual curiosity or human sympathy could fail to be stirred by the arguments of Enda McDonagh, Gabriel Daly, Fergal O'Connor or Margaret McCurtain.

I may be accused of dwelling unduly on the 1960s here. But it was in the 1960s that it finally seemed we were about to lose the habit of waiting until our backs were to the wall before entering a serious discussion about what was to be done.

And it was in the middle to late 1960s that we began to ask whether we had used our independence well, just as our contemporaries in Northern Ireland began to ask whether it was possible for people there to reform Northern Ireland without an appeal to tribalism or resort to violence.

These were political questions, of concern not only to party organisers, vested interests and controlling elites, but to the public at large and especially those who would be directly affected by such change as the electorate considered necessary.

But the political system isn't always a match for changes in other areas. As industrial development progressed, so did the opportunity to cash in on its profits, especially where the interests of property and politics coincided.

Someone had to pay. And they did: usually those who could least afford it – the poorest of the poor.

We joined the European Community (the EEC as it was); and we've had rich returns for our shared sovereignty. But it has taken us 30 years to hold our most thorough debate on Ireland's role in the EU and what Europe means to us.

But industrialisation which is not matched by social development is, as the European social democrats should have taught us, a cold comfort. In our richest years, when we had the chance to make this a fairer and more civilised place to live in, we didn't take it. If our backs were to be against the wall again, we would not be prepared for it.

Everyone knows how untrustworthy people find the Dáil and the Government. But, as Michael Mills pointed out the other day, the media must share responsibility for our political failures.

It's ironic that he should have become an Ombudsman for this State but the newspaper industry should fail to provide an Ombudsman of its own.

Finally, thanks to the readers; comradely wishes to my colleagues and to the new leader of the Labour Party.

And, to one and all, this question: do we have to wait until our backs are to the wall again and Irish society is about to fall apart before challenging the latest orthodoxy – that market forces will solve everything?

They won't, you know.

Afterword by Geraldine Kennedy

I MET DICK Walsh on my first day in *The Irish Times* in February 1973. He was a giant in journalism but, even then, always found time to encourage cub reporters.

He never changed over the years.

I marvelled when I was young at the detail of Dick's knowledge about historical events. I wondered if I would ever be in the honoured position as a reporter to have my own personal insight into the happenings making history. Dick's big story as a journalist was the coverage of the Arms Crisis in 1970 and, like most of his contemporaries in the political correspondents' room in Leinster House, he came down unambiguously on one side. He never wavered in his admiration for Jack Lynch and Des O'Malley from that time.

Dick was a loyal friend and a fierce enemy. He hated humbug. He loved politics, people and a sense of place. He always sided with the small person. Though he lived in Dublin for most of his life, he never ceased to be a Clareman. He brought his own unique insight as a countryman to the national affairs in the capital.

Throughout the interwoven phases of his life, Dick was a fearless champion of the causes he espoused: parliamentary democracy, social justice, equality and the right of the individual against the State. He was passionate about standards in journalism.

He took a pioneering interest in the exposure of corruption in all areas of public life.

Above all else, Dick loved literary words and the colloquial turn of phrase. He loved good conversation. He could travel through the world of politics and literature on the telephone in later years – when he had been become severely disabled by a debilitating illness.

He had a great spirit. His kindness knew no bounds. He was also great fun.

He gave generously of his time to the profession of journalism. He was nominated as a Member of Honour of the National Union of Journalists last year. He pioneered the establishment of the Editorial Committee within *The Irish Times* which is concerned with the editorial and ethical integrity of the newspaper.

Dick Walsh was an institution within two institutions: *The Irish Times* and the Oireachtas. It is a measure of his stature in the world of politics that a moment's silence was observed in the Dáil and Seanad as a tribute to him on his death.

Dick was the chronicler of major public events over 40 years. And his uniquely original verdict on those happenings were written in his Saturday columns in the newspaper. Love him or hate him, they were compulsive reading from the finest commentator of his generation.

Geraldine Kennedy
Editor, *The Irish Times*